THE HEART OF
THE ENLIGHTENED

THE HEART OF THE ENLIGHTENED

A Book of Story Meditations

Anthony de Mello, S.J.

Doubleday

NEW YORK LONDON TORONTO SYDNEY AUCKLAND

Published by DOUBLEDAY, a division of
Bantam Doubleday Dell Publishing Group, Inc.,
666 Fifth Avenue, New York, New York 10103

DOUBLEDAY and the portrayal of an anchor with a dolphin
are trademarks of Doubleday, a division of
Bantam Doubleday Dell Publishing Group, Inc.

Originally published in India by Gujarat Sahitya Prakash

This edition published by special arrangement with the
Center for Spiritual Exchange

Library of Congress Cataloging-in-Publication Data
De Mello, Anthony, 1931–1987
The heart of the enlightened : a book of
  story-meditations
Anthony de Mello.
    p.   cm.
    1. Meditations.   I. Title.
BX2182.2.D387   1989   88-23417
242—dc19   CIP

ISBN 0-385-24672-2

CONTENTS

Warning

It is a great mystery that though the human heart longs for Truth in which alone it finds liberation and delight, the first reaction of human beings to Truth is one of hostility and fear. So the Spiritual Teachers of humanity, like Buddha and Jesus, created a device to circumvent the opposition of their listeners: the story. They knew that the most entrancing words a language holds are "Once upon a time . . . ," that it is common to oppose a truth but impossible to resist a story. Vyasa, the author of the Mahabharata, says that if you listen carefully to a story you will never be the same again. That is because the story will worm its way into your heart and break down barriers to the divine. Even if you read the stories in this book only for the entertainment there is no guarantee that an occasional story will not slip through your defenses and explode when you least expect it to. So you have been warned!

If you are foolhardy enough to court enlightenment, this is what I suggest you do:

A. Carry a story around in your mind so you can dwell on it in leisure moments. That will give it a chance to work on your subconscious and reveal its hidden meaning. You will then be surprised to see how it comes to you quite unexpectedly just when you need it to light up an event or situation and bring you insight and inner healing. That is when you will realize that, in exposing yourself to these stories, you were auditing a Course in Enlightenment for which no guru is needed other than yourself!

B.   Since each of these stories is a revelation of Truth, and since Truth, when spelled with a capital *t,* means the truth about *you,* make sure that each time you read a story you single-mindedly search for a deeper understanding of yourself. Read it the way one would read a medical book—wondering if one has any of the symptoms; and not a psychology book—thinking what typical specimens one's friends are. If you succumb to the temptation of seeking insight into others, the stories will do you damage.

So passionate was Mullah Nasruddin's love for truth that he traveled to distant places in search of Koranic scholars and he felt no inhibitions about drawing infidels at the bazaar into discussions about the truths of his faith.

One day his wife told him how unfairly he was treating her—and discovered that her husband had no interest whatsoever in that kind of Truth!

It's the only kind that matters, of course. Ours would be a different world, indeed, if those of us who are scholars and ideologues, whether religious or secular, had the same passion for self-knowledge that we display for our theories and dogmas.

❧

"Excellent sermon," said the parishioner, as she pumped the hand of the preacher. "Everything you said applies to someone or other I know."

See?

Instruction

The stories are best read in the order in which they are set out here. Read no more than one or two at a time—that is, if you wish to get anything more than entertainment from them.

Note

The stories in this book come from a variety of countries, cultures, and religions. They belong to the spiritual heritage —and popular humor—of the human race.

All that the author has done is string them together with a specific aim in mind. His task has been that of the weaver and the dyer. He takes no credit at all for the cotton and the thread.

SPIRITUALITY

Given the nature of the spiritual quest . . .

A man came upon a tall tower and stepped inside to find it all dark. As he groped around, he came upon a circular staircase. Curious to know where it led to, he began to climb, and as he climbed, he sensed a growing uneasiness in his heart. So he looked behind him and was horrified to see that each time he climbed a step, the previous one fell off and disappeared. Before him the stairs wound upward and he had no idea where they led; behind him yawned an enormous black emptiness.

. . . true seekers are rare . . .

When the King visited the monasteries of the great Zen master Lin Chi, he was astonished to learn that there were more than ten thousand monks living there with him.

Wanting to know the exact number of the monks, the King asked, "How many disciples do you have?"

Lin Chi replied, "Four or five at the very most."

❧

. . . imposters many . . .

A couple on their honeymoon were about to get into bed at their hotel when a masked burglar broke in. He drew a chalk circle on the floor, beckoned to the husband, and said, "Stand there in that circle. If you step out of it I shall shoot you through the head."

While the husband stood there bolt upright, the burglar took everything he could lay his hands on, threw it all into a sack, and was about to get away when he saw the pretty bride covered in nothing more than a sheet. He beckoned to her, turned on the radio, made her dance with him, hugged her, kissed her—and would have raped her if she hadn't valiantly fought him off.

When the burglar finally took off, the woman turned to her husband and yelled, "What kind of man are you that you stood there in the middle of that circle doing nothing while I was almost raped!"

"It isn't true to say that I did nothing," the man protested.

"Well, what did you do?"

"I defied him. Each time he had his back turned toward me, I stuck my foot out of the circle!"

The kind of danger we are ready for is the kind we can face from a safe distance.

After thirty years of watching television, a husband said to his wife, "Let's do something really exciting tonight."

Instantly she conjured up visions of a night in town. "Great!" she said. "What shall we do?"

"Well, let's exchange chairs."

In a little frontier town there was an old man who had lived in the same house for fifty years.

One day he surprised everyone by moving into the house next door. Reporters from the local papers descended on him to ask him why he had moved.

"I guess it was the gypsy in me," he replied with a self-satisfied smile.

Have you heard of the man who accompanied Christopher Columbus on his expedition to the New World and kept worrying the whole time that he might not get back in time to succeed the old village tailor and someone else might snatch the job?

To succeed in the adventure called spirituality one must have one's mind set on getting the most out of life. Most people settle for trifles such as wealth, fame, comfort, and human company.

A man was so enamored of fame he was ready to hang on a gibbet if that would get his name in the headlines. Is there really a difference between him and most businesspeople and politicians? (Not to mention the rest of us who set such store by public opinion.)

. . . for the one essential is lacking.

According to an ancient Indian fable, a mouse was in constant distress because of its fear of the cat. A magician took pity on it and turned it into a cat. But then it became afraid of the dog. So the magician turned it into a dog. Then it began to fear the panther. So the magician turned it into a panther. Whereupon it was full of fear for the hunter. At this point the magician gave up. He turned it into a mouse again saying, "Nothing I do for you is going to be of any help because you have the heart of a mouse."

A priest walked into a pub, indignant to find so many of his parishioners there. He rounded them up and shepherded them into the church.

Then he solemnly said, "All those who want to go to heaven, step over here to the left." Everyone stepped over except one man, who stubbornly stood his ground.

The priest looked at him fiercely and said, "Don't you want to go to heaven?"

"No," said the man.

"Do you mean to stand there and tell me you don't want to go to heaven when you die?"

"Of course, I want to go to heaven when I die. I thought you were going now!"

We are ready to go all the way—only when our brakes don't work.

∿

The Buddhist nun called Ryonen was born in the year 1779. The famous Japanese warrior, Shingen, was her grandfather. She was considered one of the loveliest women in the whole of Japan and a poetess of no mean talent, so already at the age of seventeen she was chosen to serve at the royal court, where she developed a great fondness for Her Imperial Majesty the Empress. Now the Empress died a sudden death and Ryonen underwent a profound spiritual experience: she became acutely aware of the passing nature of all things. That was when she made up her mind to study Zen.

But her family wouldn't hear of it. They practically forced her into marriage but not before she had extracted from them and from her future husband the promise that after she had borne him three children she would be free to become a nun. This condition was fulfilled when she was twenty-five. Then neither the pleas of her husband nor anything else in the world could dissuade her from the task she had set her heart on. She shaved her head, took the name of Ryonen (which means "to understand clearly"), and set out on her quest.

She came to the city of Edo and asked the Master Tetsu-gyu to accept her as his disciple. He took one look at her and rejected her because she was too beautiful. So she went to another master, Hakuo. He rejected her for the same reason: her beauty, he said, would only be a source of trouble. So Ryonen branded her face with a red-hot iron, thereby destroying her physical beauty forever. When she came back into Hakuo's presence, he accepted her as a disciple.

Ryonen wrote a poem on the reverse side of a little mirror to commemorate the occasion:

> As a handmaid of my Empress
> I burnt incense
> to give fragrance to my lovely clothes.
> Now as a homeless beggar
> I burn my face
> to enter the world of Zen.

When she knew her time had come to depart this world, she wrote another poem:

> Sixty-six times have these eyes beheld
> the loveliness of Autumn . . .
> Ask no more.
> Only listen to the sound of the pines
> when no wind stirs.

Once upon a time in a concentration camp there lived a prisoner who, even though he was under sentence of execution, was fearless and free. One day he was seen in the middle of the prison square playing his guitar. A large crowd gathered to listen, for under the spell of the music, they became as fearless as he. When the prison authorities saw this, they forbade the man to play.

But the next day there he was again, singing and playing on his guitar with a larger crowd around him. The guards angrily dragged him away and had his fingers chopped off.

Next day he was back, singing and making what music he could with his bleeding fingers. This time the crowds were cheering. The guards dragged him away again and smashed his guitar.

The following day he was singing with all his heart. What a song! So pure and uplifting! The crowd joined in, and while the singing lasted, their hearts became as pure as his and their spirits as invincible. So angry were the guards this time that they had his tongue torn out. A hush descended on the camp, a something that was deathless.

To the astonishment of everyone, he was back at his place the next day swaying and dancing to a silent music that no one but he could hear. And soon everyone was holding hands and dancing around this bleeding, broken figure in the center while the guards stood rooted to the ground in wonder.

Sudha Chandran, a contemporary classical Indian dancer, was cut off in the prime of her dancing career—quite literally—when her right leg had to be amputated. After she had been fitted with an artificial leg, she went back to dancing and, incredibly, made it right back to the top again. When asked how she had managed it, she said quite simply, "You don't need feet to dance."

A miser hid his gold at the foot of a tree in his garden. Every week he would dig it up and look at it for hours. One day a thief dug up the gold and made off with it. When the miser next came to gaze upon his treasure, all he found was an empty hole.

The man began to howl with grief so his neighbors came running to find out what the trouble was. When they found out, one of them asked, "Did you use any of the gold?"

"No," said the miser. "I only looked at it every week."

"Well, then," said the neighbor, "for all the good the gold did you, you might just as well come every week and gaze upon the hole."

It is not by our money but by our capacity for enjoyment that we are rich or poor. To strive for wealth and have no capacity for enjoyment is to be like the bald man who struggles to collect combs.

❧

A reporter was attempting to get a human interest story out of a very, very old man in a government-run home for the aged.

"Grandpa," said the young reporter, "how would you feel if you suddenly got a letter telling you that a distant relative had left you ten million dollars?"

"Son," said the old man slowly, "I would still be ninety-five years old, wouldn't I?"

❧

Two jewel merchants arrived at a caravanserai in the desert at about the same time one night. Each was quite conscious of the other's presence, and while unloading his camel, one of them could not resist the temptation to let a large pearl fall to the ground as if by accident. It rolled in the direction of the other who, with affected graciousness, picked it up and returned it to its owner saying, "That is a fine pearl you have there, sir. As large and lustrous as they come."

"How gracious of you to say so," said the other. "As a matter of fact, that is one of the smaller gems in my collection."

A bedouin who was sitting by the fire and had observed this drama, rose and invited the two of them to eat with him. When they began their meal, this is the story he told them:

"I, too, my friends, was, once upon a time, a jeweler like

you. One day I was overtaken by a great storm in the desert. It buffeted me and my caravan this way and that till I was separated from my entourage and lost my way completely. Days passed and I was panic-stricken to realize that I was really wandering about in circles with no sense of where I was or which direction to walk in. Then, almost dead with starvation, I unloaded every bag on my camel's back, anxiously searching through them for the hundredth time. Imagine my excitement when I came upon a pouch that had escaped my notice before. With trembling fingers I ripped it open hoping to find something to eat. Imagine my disillusionment when I found that all it contained was pearls!"

꙲

A Sufi of forbidding appearance arrived at the doors of the palace. No one dared to stop him as he made his way right up to the throne on which the saintly Ibrahim ben Adam sat.

"What is it you want?" asked the King.

"A place to sleep in this caravanserai."

"This is no caravanserai. This is my palace."

"May I ask who owned this place before you?"

"My father. He is dead."

"And who owned it before him?"

"My grandfather. He is dead too."

"And this place where people lodge for a brief while and move on—did I hear you say it was not a caravanserai?"

Everyone's in the departure lounge!

❧

A miser had accumulated five hundred thousand dinars and looked forward to a year of pleasant living before he made up his mind how best to invest his money, when suddenly the Angel of Death appeared before him to take his life away.

The man begged and pleaded and used a thousand arguments to be allowed to live a little longer, but the angel was obdurate. "Give me three days of life and I shall give you half my fortune," the man pleaded. The angel wouldn't hear of it and began to tug at him. "Give me just one day, I beg of you, and you can have everything I accumulated through so much sweat and toil." The angel was adamant still.

He was able to wring just one little concession from the angel—a few moments in which to write down this note: "Oh you, whoever you are that happen to find this note, if you have enough to live on, don't waste your life accumulating fortunes. Live! My five hundred thousand dinars could not buy me a single hour of life!"

When millionaires die and people ask, "How much did they leave?" the answer is, of course, "Everything."

And sometimes, "They didn't leave it. They were taken away from it."

The Indian mystic Ramakrishna used to say:

God laughs on two occasions. He laughs when he hears a physician say to a mother, "Don't be afraid. I shall cure the boy." God says to himself, "I am planning to take the life of the child and this man thinks he can save it!"

He also laughs when he sees two brothers divide their land by means of a boundary line saying, "This side belongs to me and the other side to you." He says to himself, "The universe belongs to me and they claim to own portions of it!"

When they came to tell a man that his house had been carried away by the flood, he laughed and said, "Impossible! I have the key to the house right here in my pocket!"

And Buddha said:

"This land is mine, these sons are mine"—such are the words of the fool who does not understand that even he is not his.

You never really possess things. You merely hold them for a while. If you are unable to give them away, you are held by them.

Whatever your treasure must be held in the hollow of your hand as water is held.

Clutch at it and it is gone.

Appropriate it to yourself and you soil it. Set it free and it is forever yours.

Here is the story a master told his disciples to show what damage a single trifling attachment can do to those who have become rich in spiritual gifts:

A villager was once riding past a cave in a mountain at the precise moment when it made one of its rare magical appearances to all who wished to enrich themselves from its treasures. He marched into the cave and found whole mountains of jewels and precious stones that he hurriedly stuffed into the saddlebags of his mule, for he knew the legend according to which the cave would be open for only a very limited period of time so its treasures had to be taken in haste.

The donkey was fully loaded and he set off rejoicing at his good fortune, when he suddenly remembered he had left his stick in the cave. He turned back and rushed into the cave. But the time for the cave to disappear had arrived and so he disappeared with it and was never seen again. After waiting for him a year or two, the villagers sold the treasure they found on the donkey and became the beneficiaries of the unfortunate man's good luck.

When the sparrow builds its nest in the forest, it occupies but a single branch. When the deer slakes its thirst at the river, it drinks no more than its belly can hold.

We collect things because our hearts are empty.

∾

There was an old Zen master called Nonoko who lived alone in a hut at the foot of a mountain. One night while Nonoko was sitting in meditation, a stranger broke into the hut and, brandishing a sword, demanded Nonoko's money. Nonoko did not interrupt his meditation while he addressed the man: "All my money is in a bowl on the shelf up there. Take all you need, but leave me five yen. I have to pay my taxes next week."

The stranger emptied the bowl of all the money it held and threw five yen back into it. He also helped himself to a precious vase he found on the shelf.

"Carry that vase with care," said Nonoko. "It will crack easily."

The stranger looked around the small barren room once more and was going to leave.

"You haven't said thank you," said Nonoko.

The man said thank you and left.

The next day the whole village was in turmoil. Many people claimed they had been robbed. Someone noticed the vase missing from the shelf in Nonoko's hut and asked if he, too, had been the victim of the burglar. "Oh, no," said Nonoko. "I gave the vase to a stranger, along with some money. He thanked me and left. He was a pleasant enough sort of fellow but a bit careless with his sword!"

A rich Muslim went to the mosque after a party and had to take off his expensive shoes and leave them outside the mosque. When he came out after prayer, the shoes were gone.

"How thoughtless of me," he said to himself. "By foolishly leaving those shoes here I was the occasion for someone to steal them. I would have gladly given them to him. Now I am responsible for creating a thief."

True philosopher that he was, Socrates believed that the wise person would instinctively lead a frugal life. He himself would not even wear shoes; yet he constantly fell under the spell of the marketplace and would go there often to look at all the wares on display.

When one of his friends asked why, Socrates said, "I love to go there and discover how many things I am perfectly happy without."

Spirituality is not knowing what you want but understanding what you do not need.

People have been known to make a rich life for themselves and others with very few possessions.

There was a group of elderly gentlemen in Japan who would meet to exchange news and drink tea. One of their diversions was to search for costly varieties of tea and create new blends that would delight the palate.

When it was the turn of the oldest member of the group to entertain the others, he served tea with the greatest ceremony, measuring out the leaves from a golden container. Everyone had the highest praise for the tea and demanded to know by what particular combination he had arrived at this exquisite blend.

The old man smiled and said, "Gentlemen, the tea that you find so delightful is the one that is drunk by the peasants on my farm. The finest things in life are neither costly nor hard to find."

The guru sat in meditation on the riverbank when a disciple bent down to place two enormous pearls at his feet, a token of reverence and devotion.

The guru opened his eyes, lifted one of the pearls, and held it so carelessly that it slipped out of his hand and rolled down the bank into the river.

The horrified disciple plunged in after it, but though he dived in again and again till late evening, he had no luck.

Finally, all wet and exhausted, he roused the guru from his meditation: "You saw where it fell. Show me the spot so I can get it back for you."

The guru lifted the other pearl, threw it into the river, and said, "Right there!"

Do not attempt to possess things, for things cannot really be possessed. Only make sure you are not possessed by them and you will be the sovereign of creation.

இ

When Buddha entered the capital of King Prasanjit, the King in person came out to him. He had been a friend of Buddha's father and had heard of the lad's renunciation. So he attempted to persuade Buddha to give up his life as a wandering beggar and return to the palace, thinking he was doing a service to his old friend.

Buddha looked into the eyes of Prasanjit and said, "Answer me truthfully. For all your outer merriment, has your kingdom brought you a single day of happiness?"

Prasanjit lowered his eyes and was silent.

There is no greater joy than to have no cause for sorrow; no greater wealth than contentment with what one has.

~&

A monkey and a hyena were walking through the forest when the hyena said, "Each time I pass by those bushes there, a lion jumps out of them and mauls me. I don't know why."

"I'll walk with you this time," said the monkey, "and side with you against the lion."

So they started to walk past the bushes when the lion pounced on the hyena and nearly mauled it to death. Meanwhile the monkey watched the proceedings from the safety of a tree that he had run up the moment the lion appeared.

"Why didn't you do something to help me?" moaned the hyena.

Said the monkey, "You were laughing so much I thought you were winning."

~&

The great Buddhist saint Nagarjuna moved around naked except for a loincloth and, incongruously, a golden begging bowl gifted to him by the King, who was his disciple.

One night he was about to lie down to sleep among the ruins of an ancient monastery when he noticed a thief lurking behind one of the columns. "Here, take this," said Nagarjuna, holding out the begging bowl. "That way you won't disturb me once I have fallen asleep."

The thief eagerly grabbed the bowl and made off—only

to return next morning with the bowl and a request. He said, "When you gave away this bowl so freely last night, you made me feel very poor. Teach me how to acquire the riches that make this kind of lighthearted detachment possible."

No one can take from you what you never took to yourself.

❧

One of Junaid's followers came to him with a purseful of gold coins.

"Have you any more gold coins?" asked Junaid.

"Yes, many more."

"And you are attached to them?"

"I am."

"Then you must keep this too, for your need is greater than mine. Since I have nothing and desire nothing, I am much wealthier than you are, you see."

The heart of the enlightened is like a mirror: it grasps nothing, refuses nothing; it receives but does not keep.

❧

A Quaker had this sign put up on a vacant piece of land next to his home: THIS LAND WILL BE GIVEN TO ANYONE WHO IS TRULY SATISFIED.

A wealthy farmer who was riding by stopped to read the sign and said to himself, "Since our friend the Quaker is so ready to part with this pilot, I might as well claim it before someone else does. I am a rich man and have all I need, so I certainly qualify."

With that he went up to the door and explained what he was there for. "And art thou truly satisfied?" the Quaker asked.

"I am, indeed, for I have everything I need."

"Friends," said the Quaker, "if thou art satisfied, what dost thou want the land for?"

While others strive for wealth, the enlightened, being content with what they have, possess it without striving.

Being well content with little, they are rich as Kings. A King himself is a pauper when his kingdom does not suffice him.

❧

King Pyrrhus of Epirus was approached by his friend Cyneas and asked, "If you conquer Rome, what will you do next, sir?"

Pyrrhus replied, "Sicily is next door and will be easy to take."

"And what shall we do after Sicily is taken?"

"Then we will move over to Africa and sack Carthage."

"And after Carthage, sir?"

"The turn of Greece will come."

"And what, may I ask, will the fruit of all these conquests be?"

"Then," said Pyrrhus, "we can sit down and enjoy ourselves."

"Can we not," said Cyneas, "enjoy ourselves now?"

The poor think they will be happy when they become rich. The rich think they will be happy when they are rid of their ulcers.

∼

A man and his wife went to visit friends in another part of the country and were taken to a racecourse. Fascinated by the sight of horses chasing one another round a track, the two of them kept betting all evening till they had no more than two dollars left.

The following day the man prevailed upon his wife to let him go to the course alone. There was a horse with a fifty-to-one odds on it in the first race. He bet on the horse and it won. He put all the money he won on another long shot in the next race and again he won. He kept doing this all evening and his entire earnings came to fifty-seven thousand dollars.

On the way back home he passed by a gambling den. An inner voice, the same that seemed to have guided him in his choice of horses, said, "Stop here and go in." So he stopped, went in, and found himself standing in front of a roulette wheel. The voice said, "Number thirteen." The man put the entire fifty-seven thousand on number thirteen. The wheel spun. The croupier announced, "Number fourteen."

So the man walked back home with nothing in his pocket. His wife called out to him from the porch, "How did it go?"

The husband shrugged his shoulders. "I lost the two dollars," he said.

Come to think of it, you never lose any more than that, no matter what you lose.

≈

Buddha seemed quite unruffled by the insults hurled at him by a visitor. When his disciples later asked him what the secret of his serenity was, he said:

"Imagine what would happen if someone placed an offering before you and you did not pick it up. Or someone sent you a letter that you refused to open; you would be unaffected by its contents, would you not? Do this each time you are abused and you will not lose your serenity."

The only kind of dignity which is genuine is that which is not diminished by the disrespect of others. You don't diminish the majesty of Niagara Falls by spitting in it.

≈

Two inmates of a deaf-and-dumb institution had a quarrel. When an official came to straighten things out between them, he found one of the men standing with his back to the other, shaking with laughter.

"What's the joke? Why is your partner here looking so angry?" the official asked, speaking with his fingers.

"Because," the mute replied, also with his fingers, "he wants to swear at me but I refuse to look!"

৵

One day Hasan of Basra saw Rabi'a al Adawiya near the riverside. Casting his prayer mat on the water, he stepped on to it and said, "O Rabi'a, come let us pray together."

Rabi'a said, "O Hasan, why have you set yourself up like a salesman in the bazaar of this world? You do this because of your weakness."

With that she threw her prayer mat into the air, flew up on it, and said, "Come up here, Hasan, so that people may see us."

But that was more than Hasan could accomplish, so he was silent. Rabi'a, wishing to gain his heart, said, "O Hasan, a fish can do what you did and a fly can do what I did. The real work lies beyond both of these; that is what we must occupy ourselves with."

৵

Buddha was once threatened with death by a bandit called Angulimal.

"Then be good enough to fulfil my dying wish," said Buddha. "Cut off the branch of that tree."

One slash of the sword, and it was done! "What now?" asked the bandit.

"Put it back again," said Buddha.

The bandit laughed. "You must be crazy to think that anyone can do that."

"On the contrary, it is you who are crazy to think that you are mighty because you can wound and destroy. That is the task of children. The mighty know how to create and heal."

The battering ram can demolish a wall; it cannot heal the breach.

੨

A visitor to an insane asylum found one of the inmates rocking back and forth in a chair cooing repeatedly in a soft, contented manner, "Lulu, Lulu . . ."

"What's this man's problem?" he asked the doctor.

"Lulu. She was the woman who jilted him," was the doctor's reply.

As they proceeded on the tour, they came to a padded cell whose occupant was banging his head repeatedly against the wall and moaning, "Lulu, Lulu . . ."

"Is Lulu this man's problem too?" asked the visitor.

"Yes," said the doctor. "He's the one Lulu finally married."

There are only two afflictions in life: not getting what you are attached to and getting what you are attached to.

A young business executive phoned his foreign representative one day and tersely announced, "I am calling to give instructions. This call will last no more than three minutes. I shall speak and you are not to interrupt. Any comments or queries you have are to be cabled to me later."

With that he went on to deliver his message. His delivery was so rapid that he finished a little ahead of time. "We have twenty seconds left," he told the man at the other end. "Have you anything to say?"

"Yes," came the reply. "You spoke so fast I couldn't understand a word."

A good way to cover less distance in more time is to go faster.

A young man came to a master and asked, "How long is it likely to take me to attain enlightenment?"

Said the master, "Ten years."

The young man was shocked. "So long?" he asked incredulously.

Said the master, "No, that was a mistake. It will take you twenty years."

The young man asked, "Why did you double the figure?"

Said the master, "Come to think of it, in your case it will probably be thirty."

Some people will never learn anything because they grasp everything too soon. Wisdom, after all, is not a station you arrive at but a manner of traveling. If you travel too fast, you will miss the scenery.

To know exactly where you're headed may be the best way to go astray. Not all those who loiter are lost.

An American preacher in Beijing asked the waiter in a restaurant what religion was for the Chinese.

The waiter took him out to the balcony and asked, "What do you see, sir?"

"I see a street and houses and people walking and buses and taxis plying."

"What else?"

"Trees."

"What else?"

"The wind is blowing."

The Chinese extended his arms and exclaimed, "That is religion, sir."

You're searching for it the way someone searches for sight with open eyes! It is so clear that it is hard to see.

~&

DISCIPLE: "What is the Tao?"
MASTER: "Everything is Tao."
DISCIPLE: "How can I get it?"
MASTER: "If you try to get it, you will miss it."

No one is ever natural who tries to be natural; or tries not to try!

~&

An old woman in China supported a monk for more than twenty years. She built him a little hut and fed him while he spent all his time in meditation.

At the end of this period she wondered what progress the man had made. She decided to put him to the test by enlisting the help of a girl aflame with desire. "Go into the hut," she told the girl, "and embrace him. Then say, 'What shall we do now?'"

The girl called on the monk at night to find him at his meditation. Without further ado, she began to caress him and said, "What are we going to do now?" The monk got into a towering rage at this impertinence. He took hold of a broom and drove the girl out of the hut.

When she got back and reported what had happened, the old woman was indignant. "To think that I fed that fellow for twenty years," she exclaimed. "He showed no understanding of your need, no disposition to guide you in your error. He need not have given in to passion; but after all these years of prayer he could at least have developed some compassion."

❧

The devotee knelt to be initiated into discipleship. The guru whispered the sacred mantra into his ear, warning him not to reveal it to anyone.

"What will happen if I do?" asked the devotee.

Said the guru, "Anyone you reveal the mantra to will be liberated from the bondage of ignorance and suffering, but you yourself will be excluded from discipleship and suffer damnation."

No sooner had he heard those words, than the devotee rushed to the marketplace, collected a large crowd around him, and repeated the sacred mantra for all to hear.

The disciples later reported this to the guru and demanded that the man be expelled from the monastery for his disobedience.

The guru smiled and said, "He has no need of anything I can teach. His action has shown him to be a guru in his own right."

❧

When Buddha first embarked upon his spiritual quest, he practiced many austerities.

One day two musicians happened to pass by the tree under which he was sitting in meditation. One was saying to the other, "Do not tighten the strings of your sitar too much or they will snap. Do not keep them too loose either or they will produce no music. Keep to the middle path."

Those words hit Buddha with such force that they revolutionized his whole approach to spirituality. He was convinced they had been said for him. From that minute on he gave up all his severities and began to follow a way that was easy and light, the way of moderation. In fact, his approach to enlightenment is called the Middle Path.

There was once a very austere man who let no food or drink pass his lips while the sun was in the heavens. In what seemed to be a sign of heavenly approval for his austerities, a bright star shone on top of a nearby mountain, visible to everyone in broad daylight, though no one knew what had brought the star there.

One day the man decided to climb the mountain. A little village girl insisted on going with him. The day was warm and soon the two were thirsty. He urged the child to drink but she said she would not unless he drank too. The poor man was in a quandary. He hated to break his fast; but he hated to see the child suffer from thirst. Finally, he drank. And the child with him.

For a long time he dared not to look up to the sky, for he feared the star had gone. So imagine his surprise when, on looking up after a while, he saw two stars shining brightly above the mountain.

EDUCATION

A family settled down for dinner at a restaurant. The waitress first took the order of the adults, then turned to the seven-year-old.

"What will you have?" she asked.

The boy looked around the table timidly and said, "I would like to have a hot dog."

Before the waitress could write down the order, the mother interrupted. "No hot dogs," she said. "Get him a steak with mashed potatoes and carrots."

The waitress ignored her. "Do you want ketchup or mustard on your hot dog?" she asked the boy.

"Ketchup."

"Coming up in a minute," said the waitress as she started for the kitchen.

There was a stunned silence when she left. Finally the boy looked at everyone present and said, "Know what? She thinks I'm real!"

"How are your children?"

"Both of them are very well, thank you."

"How old are they?"

"The doctor is three and the lawyer is five."

❧

Little Mary was on the beach with her mother.

"Mummy, may I play in the sand?"

"No, darling. You'll only soil your clean clothes."

"May I wade in the water?"

"No. You'll get wet and catch a cold."

"May I play with the other children?"

"No. You'll get lost in the crowd."

"Mummy, buy me an ice cream."

"No. It's bad for your throat."

Little Mary began to cry.

Mother turned to a woman who was standing nearby and said, "For heaven's sake! Have you ever seen such a neurotic child?"

❧

A man began to give large doses of cod-liver oil to his Doberman because he had been told that the stuff was good for dogs. Each day he would hold the head of the protesting dog between his knees, force its jaws open, and pour the liquid down its throat.

One day the dog broke loose and spilled the oil on the floor. Then, to the man's great surprise, it returned to lick the spoon. That is when he discovered that what the dog had been fighting was not the oil but his method of administering it.

❧

An ancient legend has it that when God was creating the world, He was approached by four angels. The first one asked, "How are you doing it?" The second, "Why are you doing it?" The third, "Can I be of help?" The fourth, "What is it worth?"

The first was a scientist; the second, a philosopher; the third, an altruist; and the fourth, a real estate agent.

A fifth angel watched in wonder and applauded in sheer delight. This one was the mystic.

❧

Little Johnny was trying out for a part in the school play. His mother knew that he had set his heart on it but she feared he would not be chosen. On the day the parts were given out, Johnny, back from school, rushed into his mother's arms, bursting with pride and excitement. "Mother," he shouted, "guess what! I've been chosen to clap and cheer."

From a child's report card: "Samuel participates very nicely in the group singing by helpful listening."

❧

One of the few men to walk on the moon tells how he had to suppress his artistic instincts when he got there.

He remembered looking back at Earth and being enraptured by the sight. For a while he stood rooted to the ground, thinking, "My, that's lovely!"

Then he quickly shook the mood off and said to himself, "Stop wasting your time and go collect rocks."

There are two educations: the one that teaches how to make a living and the one that teaches how to live.

❧

Andrew Carnegie, one of the richest men in the world, was once asked, "You could have stopped any time, couldn't you, because you always had much more than you needed."

He replied, "Yes, that's right. But I could not stop. I had forgotten how to."

Many fear that if they stopped to think and wonder, they might not be able to get started again.

❧

An old man had lived most of his life on what was considered to be one of the loveliest islands in the world. Now that he had returned to spend his retirement years in the big city, someone said to him, "It must have been wonderful to live for so many years on an island that is considered one of the wonders of the world."

The old man gave that some thought, then said, "Well,

to tell you the truth, if I had known it was so famous, I'd have looked at it."

People don't need to be taught how to look. They merely need to be saved from schools that blind them.

In the early 1850s American painter James McNeill Whistler spent a brief—and academically unsuccessful—period at West Point, the U.S. Military Academy. The story goes that when he was assigned to draw a bridge, he drew a romantic stone one, complete with grassy banks and two small children fishing from it. "Get those children off that bridge!" said the instructor. "This is an engineering exercise."

Whistler got the kids off the bridge, drew them fishing from the bank of the river, and resubmitted the drawing. The angry instructor yelled, "I told you to remove those children. Get them completely out of the picture!"

But the creative urge was too strong in Whistler. His next version had the children "completely out of the picture" indeed. They were buried under two small tombstones on the riverbank.

Noticing that his father was growing old, the son of a burglar said, "Father, teach me your trade so that when you retire I may carry on the family tradition."

The father did not reply but that night he took the boy along with him to break into a house. Once inside, he opened a closet and asked his son to find out what was inside. No sooner had the lad stepped in than the father slammed the door shut and bolted it, making such a noise in the process that the whole house was awakened. Then he himself slipped quietly away.

Inside the closet the boy was terrified, angry, and puzzled as to how he was going to make his escape. Then an idea came to him. He began to make a noise like a cat; whereupon a servant lit a candle and opened the closet to let the cat out. The boy jumped out as soon as the closet door opened and everyone gave chase. Observing a well beside the road, he threw a large stone into it and hid in the shadows; then he stole away while his pursuers peered into the depths, hoping to see the burglar drown.

Back home again the boy forgot his anger in his eagerness to tell his story. But his father said, "Why tell me the tale? You are here. That is enough. You have learned the trade."

Education should not be a preparation for life; it should be life.

A group of college students begged novelist Sinclair Lewis to give them a lecture, explaining that all of them were to become writers themselves.

Lewis began with: "How many of you really intend to be writers?" All hands were raised.

"In that case, there is no point in my talking. My advice to you is: go home and write, write, write . . ."

With that, he returned his notes to his pocket and left the room.

❧

With the help of a manual of instructions, a woman tried for hours to assemble a complicated new appliance she had recently bought. She finally gave up and left the pieces all over the kitchen table.

Imagine her surprise when she got back several hours later to find the machine put together by the housemaid and functioning perfectly.

"How on earth did you do that?" she exclaimed.

"Well, ma'am, when you don't know how to read, you're forced to use your brains," was the serene reply.

❧

A man who had just retired from forty-seven years of work as a reporter and editor phoned the local education board and, after explaining his background in the newspaper business, said he would like to get involved in the local literacy program.

There was a long pause. Then someone at the other end said, "That would be fine. But would you want to teach or to learn?"

Three boys accused of stealing watermelons were brought to court and faced the judge nervously, expecting the worst, for he was known to be a severe man.

He was also a wise educator. With a rap of his gavel he said, "Any man in here who never stole a single watermelon when he was a boy, raise his hand." He waited. The court officials, policemen, spectators—and the judge himself—kept their hands on the desks in front of them.

When he was satisfied that not a single hand was raised in the court, the judge said, "Case dismissed."

Religious-minded woman mourning the ways of the younger generation: "It's because of the cars! Look how far they can go for a dance or a date nowadays. It wasn't that way in your day, was it, Grandma?"

Eighty-seven-year-old lady: "Well, we certainly went as far as we could."

MOTHER: "Did you know that God was present when you stole that cookie from the kitchen?"
CHILD: "Yes."
MOTHER: "And he was looking at you all the time?"
CHILD: "Yes."

MOTHER: "And what do you think he was saying to you?"
CHILD: "He was saying, 'There's no one here but the two of us—take two.'"

⬦

When the young rabbi succeeded his father, everyone began to tell him how completely unlike his father he was.

"On the contrary," replied the young man. "I'm exactly like the old man. He imitated no one. I imitate no one."

Be yourself! Beware of imitating the behavior of the great if you do not have the inner disposition that inspired them to act.

⬦

When Handel's *Messiah* was first performed in London, the King, who was present, was so carried away by religious sentiment during the "Hallelujah" chorus that, against all convention, he stood up in silent respect for the masterpiece he was hearing.

When they saw this, all the nobles present followed the example of the King and stood up too. That was the signal, of course, for everyone in the audience to stand up!

Since then it is considered de rigueur to stand up each time the "Hallelujah" is sung regardless of one's inner disposition or the quality of the performance.

❧

An old sailor gave up smoking when his pet parrot developed a persistent cough. He was worried that the pipe smoke that frequently filled the room had damaged the parrot's health.

He had a vet examine the bird. After a thorough checkup the vet concluded that the parrot did not have psittacosis or pneumonia. It had merely been imitating the cough of its pipe-smoking master.

❧

Uncle Joe had come for the weekend and little Jimmy was ecstatic that his great hero was going to share his room and bed.

Just after lights out, Jimmy remembered something. "Oops!" he cried, "I nearly forgot!"

He jumped out of bed and knelt down beside it. Not wishing to set a bad example to the little fellow, Uncle Joe heaved himself out of bed and knelt down on the other side.

"Boy!" whispered Jimmy in awe. "When Mom finds out tomorrow, you'll get it! The pot's on this side."

≈

"I wish you would dress more in accordance with your position. I'm sorry you have allowed yourself to become so shabby."

"But I am not shabby."

"Yes, you are. Take your grandfather. He was always so elegantly dressed. His clothes were expensive and well tailored."

"Ha! I've got you there! These are my grandfather's clothes I am wearing!"

≈

A philosopher who had only one pair of shoes asked the cobbler to repair them for him while he waited.

"It's closing time," said the cobbler, "so it won't be possible for me to repair them just now. Why don't you come for them tomorrow?"

"I have only one pair of shoes and it won't be possible for me to walk without shoes."

"Very well, I shall lend you a used pair for the day."

"What! Wear someone else's shoes? What do you take me for?"

"Why should you object to having someone else's shoes on your feet when you don't mind carrying other people's ideas in your head?"

❧

"What did you have in school today?" a father asked his teenage son.

"Oh, we had lectures on sex," was the reply.

"Lectures on sex? What did they tell you?"

"Well, first there was a priest who told us why we shouldn't. Then a doctor told us how we shouldn't. Finally the principal gave us a talk on where we shouldn't."

❧

The Dean of Women was introducing the newcomers to a college and thought fit to touch on the subject of sex morality.

"In moments of temptation, ask yourself just one question: Is an hour of pleasure worth a lifetime of shame?"

At the end of the lecture she asked if there were any questions. One of the girls timidly raised her hand and said, "Could you tell us how you make it last one hour?"

❧

U.S. President William Howard Taft was at dinner one night when his youngest son made a disrespectful remark about his father.

Everyone was shocked at the audacity of the boy and a hush descended on the room.

"Well," said Mrs. Taft, "aren't you going to punish him?"

"If the remark was addressed to me as his father, he will certainly be punished," said Taft. "But if he addressed it to the President of the United States, that is his constitutional privilege."

Why should a father be exempt from criticism that's good for a President?

❧

A guru was holding class for a group of young disciples when they begged him to reveal to them the Sacred Mantra by which the dead are restored to life.

"What would you do with a dangerous thing like that?" the guru asked.

"Nothing. It would just serve to strengthen our faith," they replied.

"Premature knowledge is a dangerous thing, my children," the old man said.

"When is knowledge premature?" they demanded.

"When it gives power to someone who does not as yet have the wisdom that must go with its use."

The disciples persisted, however, so the holy man, in spite of himself, whispered the Sacred Mantra into their ears, imploring them repeatedly to use it with the greatest discretion.

Not long afterward the young men were walking along a desert place where they saw a heap of bleached bones. In the spirit of frivolity that generally accompanies a crowd, they decided to test the Mantra, which should only have been used after prolonged meditation.

No sooner had they uttered the magic words than the bones gained flesh and were transformed into ravenous wolves, which chased them and tore them to shreds.

~

At the age of sixty-one Master Soyen Shaku passed from this world, but not before he had fulfilled his appointed task—he left for posterity a more varied and more sublime teaching than that of most Zen masters. It was said that his pupils would sometimes sleep after the midday meal, overcome with lassitude in the summer. Even though he himself never wasted a minute, Soyen never said a word about this failing in his disciples.

At the age of twelve he was already studying the philosophical tenets of the Tendai school. One summer day the heat was so oppressive that little Soyen, observing that his teacher was away, stretched out and fell into a deep sleep that lasted three hours. He woke up, with a start, when he heard the master enter, but it was too late—there he lay, sprawled across the doorway.

"Please excuse me, please excuse me," his teacher whispered as he stepped reverently over Soyen's prostrate body as if it were the body of some distinguished guest. After that Soyen never again slept in the daytime.

❧

A little boy running down the street turned a corner suddenly and collided with a man. "My goodness!" said the man. "Where are you off to in such a hurry?"

"Home," said the lad. "And I'm in a hurry because my mother is going to spank me."

"Are you so eager to be spanked that you are running home for it?" asked the astonished stranger.

"No. But if Father gets home before me, he will do the spanking."

Children are mirrors. When they are in the presence of love, that's what they reflect. When love is absent, they have nothing to give out.

❧

Nasruddin handed a boy a pitcher and told him to go fetch water from the well. Before the child set out, however, he clouted him on the ear and shouted, "Mind you don't drop it!"

An onlooker said, "How can you strike a poor child before he has done anything wrong?"

Said Nasruddin, "I suppose you would prefer me to strike him *after* he has broken the pitcher, when both the pitcher and the water are lost? When I clout him he remembers, and so the pot and the water are saved."

❧

A despairing couple sent urgently for the child psychologist because they just did not know what to do with their little son, who had installed himself on the rocking horse of a neighboring child and refused to get off. He had three rocking horses of his own at home, but he was adamant that the one he wanted to sit on was *this* one. Attempts to drag him away led to such howls and shrieks that he was put right back on the horse.

The psychologist first settled the matter of his fee, then walked up to the boy, tousled his hair affectionately, bent down, and smilingly whispered something in his ear. Instantly the boy got off the horse and docilely followed his parents home.

"What kind of magic did you use on the child?" asked the wondering parents. The psychologist collected his fee before he said, "Simple. I just bent down and said, 'If you don't get off that horse this minute, I'm going to beat you up so you won't be able to sit down for another week. I'm being paid to do this, so I mean it.'"

Before you punish a child, ask yourself if you are not the cause of the offense.

❧

PARENTS: "Why is it that though Johnny is younger than you, his marks at school are always better?"
SEVEN-YEAR-OLD: "Because Johnny's parents are clever."

The modern child:

A man wanted to foster a love for music in his children so he bought them a piano.

When he got home, he found them contemplating the piano in puzzlement. "How," they asked, "do you plug it in?"

A little boy was in a village, away from the big city for the first time in his life. He was standing on the sidewalk when an old man drove up in a horse cart and went into a shop. The boy kept gazing in wonder at the horse, an animal he had never seen in his life. When the old man came out of the shop and was preparing to drive away, the boy said, "Hey, mister! Maybe I ought to warn you that he just lost his gasoline!"

A little girl stood in a fruit store with a banana peel in her hand.

"What is it you want, darling?" said the vendor.

"A refill," was the reply.

๛

The master at the school for archery was known to be a master of life just as much as of archery.

One day his brightest pupil scored three bull's-eyes in a row at a local contest. Everyone went wild with applause. Congratulations poured in for pupil—and master.

The master, however, seemed unimpressed. Even critical.

When the pupil later asked him why, he said, "You have yet to learn that the target is not the target."

"What *is* the target?" the pupil demanded to know.

But the master would not say. This was something the boy would have to learn on his own someday, for it could not be communicated in words.

One day the pupil discovered that what he was meant to aim at was not achievement but attitude; not the bull's-eye, but the disappearance of the ego.

๛

A teacher learned to become a wise and compassionate educator the hard way, by making many mistakes. Here is one of them:

He was the principal of a school when a lad came to say he wanted to leave for another school.

"Why, son? What's wrong? What makes you unhappy? Your marks are good."

"Nothing's wrong, sir. I just want to leave."

"Is it the teachers? Is there any teacher you do not like?"

"No, sir. It isn't the teachers."

"Is it the other students? Have you had a fight with someone?"

"No. It's nothing like that."

"Is it the fees? Are they too high?"

"No, sir. It isn't that either."

The principal then paused for a long while, confident that by his silence he would get the lad to speak. Suddenly the boy was wiping tears from his eyes. The principal knew he had won. In his softest, most understanding tone he said, "You're crying because something is bothering you, aren't you?"

The boy nodded.

"Well then, tell me why you are crying."

The boy looked straight at the principal and said, "Because you are asking me all these questions."

There was a question of opening a reformatory for boys and a well-known educator was called in for advice. He made a passionate plea for humane methods of education at the reformatory, urging the founders to spare no expense in getting the services of kindhearted and competent educators.

He concluded by saying, "If only one boy is saved from moral depravity, it will justify all the cost and labor invested in an institution like this."

Later a member of the board said to him, "Didn't you get just a wee bit carried away there? Would all the cost and labor be justified if we could save only one boy?"

"If it were my boy, yes!" was the reply.

AUTHORITY

AUTHORITY

A tale from the Calcutta mystic Ramakrishna:

There was a King who used to have the Bhagavad Gita recited to him every day by a priest. The priest would then explain the text and say, "O King, have you understood what I have said?"

And every day the King would say neither yes nor no. He would only say, "You had better understand it first yourself."

This always caused sorrow to the poor priest, who had spent hours preparing the daily lesson for the King and knew that his explanation was lucid and clear.

Now the priest was a sincere seeker after Truth. While he was meditating one day he suddenly saw the illusory nature—the relative reality—of all things: house, family, wealth, friends, honor, reputation, and everything else. So clearly did he see this that all desire for these things vanished in his heart. He decided to leave home and take up the life of a wandering ascetic.

Before he left home, he sent the King this message: "O King! At last I have understood."

A woman was afflicted with a bad cold and nothing the doctor prescribed seemed to give her any relief.

"Can you do nothing to cure me, Doctor?" she asked in frustration.

"I have a suggestion," said the doctor. "Go home and have a hot shower, then before drying yourself, stand stark naked in a draft."

"Will that cure me?" she asked, surprised.

"No, but it will give you pneumonia. And that I can cure."

Has it ever occurred to you that your guru might be offering you the remedy for an illness that he himself was the cause of?

"Thank God we took a mule with us on the picnic because when one of the boys was injured we used the mule to carry him back."

"How did he get injured?"

"The mule kicked him."

"Could you recommend a good doctor?"

"I suggest Dr. Chung. He saved my life."

"How did that happen?"

"Well, I had this serious illness and went to see Dr. Ching. I took his medicine and felt worse. So I went to Dr. Chang. I took his medicine and felt like I was dying. So I finally went to Dr. Chung—and he wasn't in."

꙳

Belief in authority endangers perception:

The doctor bent over the lifeless figure in bed. Then he straightened up and said, "I am sorry to say that your husband is no more, my dear."

A feeble sound of protest came from the lifeless figure in bed: "No, I'm still alive."

"Hold your tongue," said the woman. "The doctor knows better than you."

꙳

A neighbor came to borrow Nasruddin's donkey.

"It's out on loan," said Nasruddin.

At that moment the animal began to bray from within its stable.

"But I can hear it bray," said the neighbor.

"So whom are you going to believe, the donkey or me?"

꙳

The crown prince was a duffer so the King employed a special tutor for him. Lessons began with a careful explanation of Euclid's first theorem.

"Is this clear, Your Royal Highness?" asked the tutor.

"No," said His Royal Highness.

So the tutor patiently went over the theorem again. "Is it clear now?"

"No," said the prince.

Once again the tutor went to work on the theorem—with no effect. When even after the tenth attempt the royal duffer could make no sense of the theorem, the poor tutor was reduced to tears. "Believe me, Your Royal Highness," he cried, "this theorem is true and this is the way it is proved."

On hearing these words, the prince rose to his feet and said with a solemn bow, "My dear sir, I have full faith in what you say, so if you assure me that the theorem is true, I wholeheartedly accept it. My only regret is that you did not give me this assurance earlier so that we could have then proceeded to the second theorem without wasting any time."

That way you have all the right answers without knowing geometry as people have all the—to them!—right beliefs without knowing God. To say to authority, "I'm dumb. Please think for me," is like saying, "I'm thirsty. Please drink for me."

Buddha says, "Monks and scholars should not accept my words out of respect but should analyze them as a goldsmith analyzes gold by cutting, melting, scraping, and rubbing it."

Tall man in movie theater to little boy sitting behind him: "Can you see the screen, son?"

"No."

"Not to worry. Just look at me and laugh every time I laugh."

❧

Marshal Ferdinand Foch was Commander of the Allied Forces during the First World War. His chauffeur, Pierre, was sedulously cultivated by newspaper reporters who hoped to get information on what was going on in the marshal's mind. They were always asking him when the war would get over. But Pierre would never say.

One day the reporters caught Pierre just as he was leaving headquarters. As they crowded around him, the chauffer said, "Today the marshal spoke."

"What did he say?" they asked eagerly.

"He said, 'Pierre, what do you think? When will the war get over?' "

A priest's daughter asked him where he got the ideas for his sermons. "From God," he replied.

"Then why do I see you scratching things out?" asked the girl.

❧

The radio genius, Marconi, sat up all night with a friend in his laboratory, discussing all the intricate aspects of wireless communication.

As they were leaving the laboratory Marconi suddenly said, "All my life I have been studying this matter but there is one thing I simply cannot understand about radio."

"Something *you* do not understand about radio!" said the astonished friend. "What is it?"

Said Marconi, "Why does it work?"

Many years ago a bishop on the East Coast of the United States paid a visit to a small religious college on the West Coast. He was lodged in the home of the college president, who was a progressive young man, a professor of physics and chemistry.

The president one day invited the members of his faculty to dinner with the bishop so they could benefit from his wisdom and experience. After dinner the talk turned to the millennium and the bishop claimed that it could not be far off. One of the reasons he adduced for this was the fact that everything in nature had been discovered and all possible inventions had been made.

The president politely demurred. In his opinion, he said, humanity was on the threshold of brilliant new discoveries. The bishop dared the president to mention one. The president said he expected that within the next fifty years or so human. would learn to fly.

This threw the bishop into a fit of laughter. "Rubbish, my dear man," he exclaimed, "if God had intended us to fly, He would have provided us with wings. Flight is reserved for the birds and the angels."

The president's name was Wright. He had two sons named Orville and Wilbur—the inventors of the first airplane.

❧

An ancient King in India sentenced a man to death. The man begged that the sentence be rescinded, and added, "If the King will be merciful and spare my life, I shall teach his horse to fly in a year's time."

"Done," said the King. "But if at the end of this period the horse cannot fly, you will be executed."

When his anxious family later asked the man how he planned to achieve this, he said, "In the course of the year the King may die. Or the horse may die. Or who knows, the horse may learn to fly!"

❧

In the presence of a guru, a young scientist was boasting of the achievements of modern science.

"We can fly, just like the birds," he was saying. "We can do what the birds can do!"

"Except sit on a barbed-wire fence," said the guru.

❧

The doctor carefully examined a patient and said, "You have had an attack of pneumonia. You are some sort of musician, aren't you?"

"Yes," said the man, surprised.

"And you play a wind instrument."

"That's right. How did you know?"

"Elementary, my dear fellow! There is a distinct straining of the lungs and the larynx is inflamed, undoubtedly because of severe pressure. Tell me, what instrument do you play?"

"The accordion."

The hazards of infallibility!

It was the birthday of the parish priest and the children had come with their birthday greetings and gifts.

Father took the gift-wrapped parcel from little Mary and said, "Ah! I see you have brought me a book." (Mary's father ran a bookstore in town.)

"Yes, how did you know?"

"Father always knows!"

"And you, Tommy, have brought me a sweater," said Father, picking up the parcel Tommy held out to him. (Tommy's father was a dealer in woolen goods.) "That's right. How did you know?" "Ah! Father always knows."

And so it went, till Father lifted Bobby's box. The wrapping paper was wet. (Bobby's father sold wines and liquors.) So Father said, "I see you have brought me a bottle of scotch and spilled some of it!" "Wrong," said Bobby, "it isn't scotch." "Well, a bottle of rum then." "Wrong again." Father's fingers were wet. He put one of them into his mouth but that gave him no clue. "Is it gin?" "No," said Bobby. "I've brought you a puppy!"

❧

Owing to a variety of circumstances, the egg of an eagle found its way to one corner of a barn where a hen was hatching her eggs. In time the little eaglet was hatched with the other chickens.

Now as time passed, the fledgling, quite unaccountably, began to experience a longing to fly. So it would say to its mother, the hen, "When shall I learn to fly?"

The poor hen was quite aware of the fact that she could not fly and hadn't the slightest notion of what other birds did to train their fledglings in the art of flight. But she was ashamed to confess to this inadequacy, so she would say, "Not yet, my child, not yet. I shall teach you when you are ready."

Months passed and the young eagle began to suspect that its mother did not know how to fly. But it could not get itself to break loose and fly on its own, for its keen longing to fly had become confused with the gratitude it experienced toward the bird that had hatched it.

❧

Going by reports he had heard of him, the Caliph appointed Nasruddin chief advisor at the court. Since his authority derived, not from competence, but from the patronage of the Caliph, Nasruddin became a danger to all who came to consult him as became evident in the following case:

"Nasruddin, you are a man of experience," said a courtier. "Do you know of a cure for aching eyes? I'm having a lot of trouble with mine."

"Let me share my own experience with you," said Nasruddin.

"I once had a toothache and got no relief till I had the tooth out."

꙳

The doctor decided that the time had come to tell his patient the truth: "I feel I should tell you that you are a very sick man and are not likely to live for more than another two days at the most. You may want to settle your affairs. Is there anyone you desire to see?"

"Yes," came the answer in a feeble voice.

"Who is it?" asked the doctor.

"Another doctor."

꙳

A young author once told Mark Twain that he was losing confidence in his ability to write. "Did you ever get that feeling yourself?" he asked.

"Yes," said Twain. "Once, after I had been writing for nearly fifteen years, it suddenly struck me that I did not possess the slightest talent for writing."

"What did you do then? Did you give up writing?"

"How could I? By then I was already famous."

❧

A rich man decided to fulfill a lifelong dream of leading an orchestra. So he hired one drummer, three saxophonists, and twenty-four violinists. At their first rehearsal he conducted so badly that the drummer invited the other musicians to leave with him. But one of the saxophonists said, "Why leave? He's paying us well. Besides, he must know something about music."

At the next rehearsal the conductor just couldn't keep time. Whereupon the drummer started to beat his drums furiously. The conductor tapped for silence, glared at the musicians, and asked, "Who did that?"

❧

A friend once told the manager of an orchestra that he would love to have a position in the orchestra. Said the manager, "I had no idea you could play an instrument."

"I can't," was the reply. "But I see you have a man there who does nothing but wave a stick around while the others play. I think I could handle his job."

❧

To please an official, Abraham Lincoln once signed an order transferring certain regiments. Secretary of War Stanton, convinced that the President had made a serious mistake, refused to carry out the order. And for good measure he added, "Lincoln is a fool!"

When this was reported to Lincoln he said, "If Stanton said I am a fool then I must be one, for he is almost always right. I think I'll step over and see for myself."

That is exactly what he did. Stanton convinced him that the order was a mistake and Lincoln promptly withdrew it. Everyone knew that part of Lincoln's greatness lay in the way he welcomed criticism.

❧

A recruit was assigned to guard the entrance to the army camp and was given instructions to let no car pass if it did not have a special pennant.

He had occasion to stop a car bearing a general, who promptly told his driver to disregard the sentry and drive on. Whereupon the recruit stepped forward, rifle at the ready, and calmly said, "Pardon me, sir, but I'm new to this. Whom do I shoot? You, sir, or the driver?"

You achieve greatness when you are oblivious of the dignity of those above you, and make those below you oblivious of yours. When you are neither haughty with the humble nor humble with the haughty.

❧

There was once a rabbi who was revered by the people as a man of God. Not a day went by when a crowd of people wasn't standing at his door seeking advice or healing or the holy man's blessing. And each time the rabbi spoke, the people would hang on his lips, drinking in his every word.

There was, however, in the audience a disagreeable fellow who never missed a chance to contradict the master. He would observe the rabbi's weaknesses and make fun of his defects to the dismay of the disciples, who began to look on him as the devil incarnate.

Well, one day the "devil" took ill and died. Everyone heaved a sigh of relief. Outwardly they looked appropriately solemn but in their hearts they were glad for no longer would the master's inspiring talks be interrupted or his behavior criticized by this disrespectful heretic.

So the people were surprised to see the master plunged in genuine grief at the funeral. When asked by a disciple later if he was mourning over the eternal fate of the dead man, he said, "No, no. Why should I mourn over our friend who is now in heaven? It was for myself I was grieving. That man was the only friend I had. Here I am surrounded by people who revere me. He was the only one who challenged me. I fear that with him gone, I shall stop growing." And as he said these words, the master burst into tears.

A woman once came to Rabbi Israel and told him her
secret sorrow: she had been married twenty years and still
had not borne a son. "What a coincidence!" said the rabbi.
"It was exactly thus with my mother." And this is the story
he told her: For twenty years his mother had had no child.
One day she heard that the holy Bal Shem Tov was in town
so she hurried to the house he was in and begged him to
pray that she might have a son. "What are you willing to
do about it?" the holy man asked. "What can I do?" she
replied. "My husband is a poor librarian but I do have
something I can offer the rabbi." With that she rushed
home, pulled a katinka out of the chest where it had been
carefully stored away, and ran back again to offer it to the
Rabbi. Now the katinka, as everyone knows, was the cape
worn by the bride on her wedding day—a precious heir-
loom handed down from one generation to another. By the
time the woman got back, the rabbi had left for another
town, so that is where she went. Being poor, however, she
had to walk the distance; by the time she got there, the
rabbi had left for another destination. Six weeks she followed after him from town to town till she finally caught
up with him. The rabbi took the katinka and gave it to the
local synagogue.

Then Rabbi Israel concluded, "My mother walked all
the way back home. A year later I was born."

"What a coincidence, indeed!" cried the woman. "I,
too, have a katinka at home. I shall bring it to you at once,

and if you offer it to the local synagogue, God will give me a son."

"Ah no, my dear," said the rabbi sadly, "that will not work. The difference between my mother and you is this: you heard her story; she had no story to go by."

After a saint has used a ladder, is is thrown away, never to be used again.

A large truck was moving through a railway underpass when it got wedged in between the road and the girders overhead. All the efforts of experts to extricate it proved useless, and traffic was stalled for miles on both sides of the underpass.

A little boy kept trying to get the attention of the foreman but was always pushed away. Finally in sheer exasperation, the foreman said, "I suppose you've come to tell us how to do this job!"

"Yes," said the child. "I suggest you let some air out of the tires."

In the layman's mind there are many possibilities. In the expert's mind there are few.

Somewhere in the 1930s a manufacturing concern in the United States sent a machine to Japan.

A month later the company received a cable: MACHINE DOES NOT WORK. SEND MAN TO FIX.

The company sent someone to Japan. Before he had the opportunity to examine the machine, the company received a second cable: MAN TOO YOUNG, SEND OLDER MAN.

The company's reply was: BETTER USE HIM. HE INVENTED MACHINE.

A centipede consulted an owl about the pain it felt in its legs.

Said the owl, "You have far too many legs! If you became a mouse, you would have only four legs—and one twenty-fourth the amount of pain."

"That's a very good idea," said the centipede. "Now show me how to become a mouse."

"Don't bother me with details of implementation," said the owl. "I only make the policy in this place."

A great painter asked a doctor friend to come and look at what he thought was his finest creation. The doctor subjected the painting to a thorough examination, taking his time over every detail. Ten minutes passed and the artist became somewhat apprehensive. "Well, what do you think?"

The doctor said, "It appears to be double pneumonia."

The dangers of trusting the expert:

A man received a note from a friend written in an illegible hand. After struggling to make sense out of it, he finally hit upon the idea of enlisting the help of the local druggist.

The man at the drugstore looked hard at the note for a whole minute, then took a large brown bottle from the shelf, placed it on the counter, and said, "That will be two dollars, please!"

A group of college students was dissatisfied with the poor quality of the beer that the cafeteria served them.

Some of them got the bright idea of pouring some in a bottle and sending it to a hospital laboratory in the hope of finding out what was in the beer.

The following day they received a note that said, "Your horse is suffering from jaundice."

A disciple once said to Confucius, "What are the basic ingredients of good government?"

He answered, "Food, weapons, and the trust of the people."

"But," continued the disciple, "if you were forced to dispense with one of these three, which would you drop?"

"Weapons."

"And if you had to drop one of the other two?"

"Food."

"But without food the people will die!"

"From time immemorial, death has been the lot of human beings. But a people that no longer trusts its rulers is lost indeed."

ॐ

When an accident deprived the village headman of the use of his legs, he took to walking on crutches. He gradually developed the ability to move with speed—even to dance and execute little pirouettes for the entertainment of his neighbors.

Then he took it into his head to train his children in the use of crutches. It soon became a status symbol in the village to walk on crutches, and before long everyone was doing so.

By the fourth generation no one in the village could walk without crutches. The village school included "Crutchery —Theoretical—Applied" in its curriculum and the village craftsmen became famous for the quality of the crutches they produced. There was even talk of developing an electronic, battery-operated set of crutches!

One day a young Turk presented himself before the village elders and demanded to know why everyone had to walk on crutches since God had provided people with legs to walk on. The village elders were amused that this upstart should think himself wiser than they so they decided to teach him a lesson. "Why don't you show us how?" they said.

"Agreed," cried the young man.

A demonstration was fixed for the following Sunday at the village square. Everyone was there when the young man hobbled on his crutches to the middle of the square, stood upright, and dropped his crutches. A hush fell on the crowd as he took a bold step forward—and fell flat on his face.

With that everyone was confirmed in their belief that it was quite impossible to walk without the help of crutches.

~~

While a wheelwright was making a wheel at the lower end of the hall, Prince Huan of Ch'i was reading a book at the upper end.

Putting aside his chisel and mallet, the wheelwright called to the prince and asked him what book he was reading.

"One that preserves the words of the sages," said the prince.

"Are those sages alive?" asked the wheelwright.

"Oh no," said the prince, "they are all dead."

"Then what you are reading can be nothing but the dirt and scum of bygone people," said the wheelwright.

"How dare you, a wheelwright, find fault with a book that I am reading? Justify your statement or you shall die."

"Well, speaking as a wheelwright," said the man, "this is how I look at the matter: When I am fashioning a wheel, if my stroke is too slow it cuts deep but is not steady; if my stroke is too fast it is steady but does not cut deep. The right pace, neither too fast nor too slow, will not get into the hand if it does not come from the heart. It is something that cannot be put into words; there is an art to it that I cannot hand on to my son. That is why I cannot let him take over my work, so here I am at the age of seventy-five still making wheels. In my opinion it must be the same with those who have gone before us. All that was worth handing on died with them; the rest they put into their books. That is why I said that what you are reading is the dirt and scum of bygone people."

In the old days it was common for people to use paper lanterns in Japan. The paper shielded a lit candle and was held together by bamboo sticks.

A blind man happened to be visiting a friend and, since it was late, was offered a lantern to take home with him.

He laughed at the suggestion. "Day and night are all one to me," he said. "What would I do with a lantern?"

His friend said, "You do not need it to find you way home, true. But it might help to prevent someone from running into you in the dark."

So the blind man started off with the lantern. It wasn't long before someone crashed into him, knocking him off balance.

"Hey, you careless fellow!" cried the blind man. "Can't you see this lantern?"

"Brother," said the stranger, "your lantern has gone out."

You walk more safely in your own darkness than in someone else's light.

HUMAN NATURE

Human beings react not to reality, but to ideas in their heads.

A group of tourists, stranded somewhere in the country-side, were given old rations to eat. Before eating the food, they tested it by throwing some of it to a dog, who seemed to enjoy it and suffered no aftereffects.

The following day they learned that the dog had died. Everyone was panic-stricken. Many began to vomit and complained of fever and dysentery. A doctor was called in to treat the victims for food poisoning.

The doctor began by asking what had happened to the body of the dog. Inquiries were made. A neighbor said casually, "Oh, it was thrown in a ditch because it got run over by a car."

Pestilence was on its way to Damascus and sped by a chief's caravan in the desert.

"Where are you speeding to?" asked the chief.

"To Damascus. I mean to take a thousand lives."

On its way back from Damascus, Pestilence passed by

the caravan again. The chief said, "It was fifty thousand lives that you took, not a thousand."

"No," said the Pestilence. "I took a thousand. It was Fear that took the rest."

They see not what is there, but what they have been trained to see.

Tommy had just got back from the beach.

"Were there other children there?" asked his mother.

"Yes," said Tommy.

"Boys or girls?"

"How could I know! They didn't have any clothes on."

Their culture and their conditioning offer them an "elevator existence."

The impatient dowager pressed the elevator button and fumed because it did not appear at once.

When it finally did, she snapped at the operator, "Where have you been?"

"Lady, where can you go in an elevator?"

~&

The walls that imprison them are mental, not real.

A bear paced up and down the twenty feet that was the length of his cage.

When, after five years, the cage was removed, the bear continued to pace up and down those twenty feet as if the cage were there. It was. For him!

~&

Two gentlemen of unsteady gait waited impatiently at the bus terminal late at night, long after the buses had ceased to ply.

A couple of hours passed before they realized, in their drunken stupor, that the last bus had gone. Seeing several buses parked at the depot, they decided to borrow one and drive themselves home.

To their disappointment, they couldn't find the bus they wanted. "Can you believe it?" said one. "A hundred buses, and not a single number 36 in the whole lot!"

"Never mind!" said the other. "Let's take a 22 up to its last stop and walk the rest of the two miles home."

~&

What they love or hate is not the essence of things or persons but only their configuration.

A young boy developed what could only be called a sand-wich phobia. Anytime he saw a sandwich, he would trem-ble and scream with fear. His mother was so upset about this, she took him to a therapist, who said, "The phobia is easily removed. Take the lad home and let him see you make a sandwich from beginning to end. This will dispel any silly notions he has about a sandwich and he'll stop trembling and screaming."

That is just what the mother did. She took two slices of bread in her hands and said, "Are you afraid of this?" The boy said, "No." She showed him the butter. Was he afraid of that? No, he wasn't. She let him see her spread the butter over the bread. Next came the lettuce. Was he afraid of that? No, he wasn't. The lettuce was placed on the bread. How about the tomato slices? Anything to be afraid of there? No, there wasn't. So those went on top of the lettuce. Any fear of the bacon strips? No fear; none at all. So those went on top of the tomato slices.

Now she held one piled-up slice in each hand and showed the slices to the boy. Still no fear. But the moment she brought the two slices together to form a sandwich, he shrieked, "Sandwich! Sandwich!" and began to tremble and be very frightened.

A young man who was blind from birth fell in love with a girl. All went well until a friend told him the girl wasn't too good-looking. At that minute he lost all interest in her. Too bad! He had been "seeing" her very well. It was his friend who was blind!

&

*Examine what they are pleased to call their free and respon-
sible behavior, and you are likely to find not conscious action, but mechanical movement . . .*

It is said that when the Great Library of Alexandria was
burned down, only one book survived. It was a very ordi-
nary book, dull and uninteresting, so it was sold for a few
pennies to a poor man who barely knew how to read.

Now that book, dull and uninteresting as it seemed, was
probably the most valuable book in the world, for on the
inside of the back cover were scrawled in large, round let-
ters, a few sentences that contained the secret of the
Touchstone—a tiny pebble that could turn anything it
touched into pure gold.

The writing declared that this precious pebble was lying
somewhere on the shore of the Black Sea among thousands
of other pebbles that were exactly like it, except in one
particular—that whereas all the other pebbles were cold to
the touch, this one was warm as if it were alive. The man
rejoiced at his good luck. He sold everything he had, borrowed a large sum of money that would last him a year, and
made for the Black Sea, where he set up his tent and began
a painstaking search for the Touchstone.

This was the way he went about it: He would lift a
pebble. If it was cold to the touch, he would not throw it
back on the shore because if he did that, he might be
lifting and feeling the same stone dozens of times. No, he

would throw it into the sea. So each day for hours on end he persevered in his patient endeavor: Lift a pebble; if it felt cold, throw it into the sea; lift another . . . and so on, endlessly.

He spent a week, a month, ten months, a whole year at this task. Then he borrowed some more money and kept at it for another two years. On and on he went: lift a pebble; hold it; feel that it was cold; throw it into the sea. Hour after hour; day after day; week after week . . . still no Touchstone.

One evening he picked up a pebble and it was warm to the touch—but through sheer force of habit, he threw it into the Black Sea!

❧

. . . *and programmed responses.*

A scientists had spent ten years researching the possibility of transforming water into petroleum. He was convinced that all he needed was one substance to effect the needed transformation, but try as he might, the formula eluded him.

One day he learned that high up in the mountains of Tibet there lived a lama who was all-knowing and could reveal to him the formula he sought.

There were three conditions, however: He had to travel there alone, and the journey was hazardous. He had to travel on foot, and the journey was arduous. And if he ever made it to the presence of the lama, he would be allowed to ask one, and only one, question.

It took him many months of hardship and danger to fulfill the first two conditions. And when he was brought into the presence of the lama, imagine his shock to find not the wizened, bearded old man he had expected but an attractive young woman, lovelier by far than anyone he could have imagined.

She smiled at him sweetly, and in a voice that to his ear sounded heavenly, she said, "Congratulations, traveler! You have made it to our mountain fastness. Now what is your question?"

To his great surprise the scientist heard himself saying, "Ma'am, may I know if you are married?"

❧

Instead of touching reality they respond to stereotypes . . .

At the final dinner of an international conference, an American delegate turned to the Chinese delegate sitting next to him, pointed to the soup, and asked, somewhat condescendingly, "Likee soupee?" The Chinese gentleman nodded eagerly.

A little later, it was, "Likee fishee?" and "Likee meatee?" and "Likee fruitee?"—and always the response was an affable nod.

At the end of the dinner the chairman of the conference introduced the guest speaker of the evening—none other than the Chinese gentleman, who delivered a penetrating,

witty discourse in impeccable English, much to the astonishment of his American neighbor.

When the speech was over, the speaker turned to his
neighbor and, with a mischievous twinkle in his eye, asked,
"Likee speechee?"

❧

. . . or rigid principles . . .

Two game hunters were involved in a lawsuit against each
other. One of them asked his lawyer if it wouldn't be a
good idea to send the judge a brace of partridges. The
lawyer was horrified. "This judge prides himself on his in-
corruptibility," he said. "A gesture like this will have just
the opposite effect from the one you intend."

After the case was over—and won—the man invited his
lawyer to dinner and thanked him for the advice concern-
ing the partridges. "I did send them to the judge, you
know," he said, "on behalf of our opponent."

Moral indignation can blind one as effectively as venality.

❧

. . . or appearances . . .

A little girl, who had been told that Lincoln wasn't very
good-looking, was taken by her father to see the President
at the White House.

Lincoln took her on his knees and chatted with her for a while in his gentle, humorous way. Suddenly the little girl called out, "Daddy! He isn't ugly at all. He's just beautiful!"

A little black boy was watching the balloon man at the Country Fair. The man was evidently a good salesman, because he allowed a red balloon to break loose and soar high up in the air, thereby attracting a crowd of prospective young customers.

Next he released a blue balloon, then a yellow on, and a white one. They all went soaring up into the sky until they disappeared. The little black boy stood looking at the black balloon for a long time, then asked, "Sir, if you sent the black one up, would it go as high as the others?"

The balloon man gave the kid an understanding smile. He snapped the string that held the black balloon in place and, as it soared upward, said, "It isn't the color, son. It's what's inside that makes it rise."

. . . or labels . . .

Isaac Goldstein ran into a cousin of his in New York.

"How are things with you?" Goldstein asked.

"Haven't you heard?" replied the cousin. "I'm a partner in the firm of Goldstein and Murphy."

"Goldstein and Murphy? Now isn't that wonderful! That's what America is all about: people of different nationalities doing business in partnership. But to you I'll confess it is something of a surprise."

"You call that a surprise? Well, I've got a bigger surprise for you. I'm Murphy."

A Russian Workers Delegation was visiting a factory in Detroit. The leader asked the foreman how many hours an American worker worked each week.

"Forty," said the foreman.

The Russian shook his head. "In my country," he said, "the average worker works sixty hours a week."

"Sixty hours?" exclaimed the foreman. "You'd never get the men in this factory to work that much. They're a bunch of Commies!"

. . . well, sometimes, anyway!

A man said to his parish priest, "My dog died yesterday, Father. Could you offer a Mass for the repose of his soul?"

The priest was outraged. "We don't offer Masses for animals here," he said sharply. "You might try the new denomination down the road. They'll probably pray for your dog."

"I really loved that little fellow," said the man, "and I'd

like to give him a decent send-off. I don't know what it is customary to offer on such occasions, but do you think five hundred thousand dollars would do?"

"Now wait a minute," said the priest. "You never told me your dog was a Catholic!"

❧

They pride themselves on their reasonableness—which they then proceed to demonstrate in astonishing ways:

A governor was visiting a state penitentiary and talking to a tramp who had asked for a pardon.

"What's the matter with this place? You're more comfortably lodged here than you have ever been, aren't you?"

"Yessir," was the reply. "But I still want to get out."

"Don't they feed you well?"

"They certainly do. That isn't it."

"Then what is it?"

"Well, sir, there's only one objection I have to this place: it's the reputation it has all over the state."

❧

A reporter asked several people in a small town if they knew the mayor.

"He's a liar and a cheat," said the gas station attendant.

"He's a pompous ass," said the schoolteacher.

"Never voted for him in my life," said the druggist.

"Most corrupt politician I've ever known," said the barber.

When the reporter finally met the mayor, he asked him what kind of salary he received.

"Good heavens, I don't get any salary," said the mayor.

"Then why did you take the job?"

"For the honor."

❧

A man at a bar turned to the stranger sitting next to him and said, "I just don't understand it. All it takes is one little drink, just one little drink to make me drunk."

"Really? Just one?"

"Yes. And it is generally the eighth one."

❧

A man in Las Vegas approached a wealthy-looking stranger and said, "Can you spare me twenty-five dollars, sir? I haven't eaten for two days and I have no place to sleep."

"How do I know you won't take the money and gamble with it?"

"No way," said the man. "Gambling money I already have with me."

❧

A couple were wondering how to dispose of five attractive puppies they had just acquired. The man drove all around town attempting to give them away but no one would have them.

They announced over the local radio that they had pedigree puppies to give away. No one seemed interested.

Finally a neighbor advised them to advertise. They went back to announce on the radio that they would sell the pups at twenty-five dollars each. Before the day was out, every one of the puppies had been sold!

❧

Two prospective buyers walked into a used car lot and began to look around. The attendant began his sales talk when one of them produced a card which said, "Sorry, we're deaf-mutes."

So the salesman pulled out a pad and began to jot down, for their benefit, all the advantages of any car they showed interest in. They finally settled on a neat little Volkswagen.

They took it around the block on a trail run and seemed so pleased that the sale was as good as made. But when they got back to the lot, they both shook their heads emphatically. No good.

The salesman scribbled on the pad, "Why? What's wrong?"

One of the men took the pad and wrote, "No radio!"

❧

When a man returned from a large city to the village of his boyhood years, one of the neighbors said to him, "I suppose you know that old Farmer Smith lost his farm?"

"No. What happened?"

"Well, one day he got the idea that his neighbor's fence was five feet into his land. He took to brooding over it. Finally he went to see a lawyer, telling him he thought this was encroachment. Well, the lawyer thought so too!"

Voltaire says, "I have never been ruined but twice: once when I lost a lawsuit and once when I won one."

It is just as astonishing to see the use they make of their imagination . . .

"If you ever marry or take a mistress after I am gone, I shall return to haunt you," said a dying woman to her husband.

So when he fell in love again some months after his wife's death, he was horrified, but not surprised, to see her ghost walk into the house one night and accuse him bitterly of infidelity.

This went on night after night till he could take it no more and went to consult a Zen master, who said, "What makes you so sure it's a ghost?"

"The fact that she knows and can describe to me every single thing I've said and done and thought and felt."

The master gave the man a bag of soybeans and said, "Make sure you do not open it, and when she appears to you tonight, ask her how many beans there are in the bag."

When the man put that question to the ghost, it fled, never to return. "Why?" the man asked the master later.

The master smiled. "Isn't it strange that your ghost knew only what you knew?" he asked.

❧

A man in Russia took his wife with him into the forest, supposedly to hunt for wolves. But when the wolves came, he ran away and abandoned her to them. The next morning he put a wreath on his door and went into mourning— but not for long, because he had a lover whom he married six months later.

The night of the wedding, his former wife appeared to him at night crying, "Help! Help! Help!" To his amazement, his new wife saw and heard nothing. Each night the woman would return and scream for help, till the man could take it no longer. One night he picked up his gun and ran after the woman, meaning to kill her a second time. She ran into the forest. He followed, stumbled, and dropped his gun. At that minute the wolves closed in on him and put an end to his life.

❧

. . . and their emotions . . .

A passenger on a train was giving the dining car waiter his order. "For dessert," he said, "I'll have tarts and ice cream."

The waiter said they had no tarts. The man exploded. "What? No tarts? That's absurd. I am one of the biggest customers this railroad has. Each year I organize trips for thousands of tourists and I have hundreds of tons of freight transported on it. And when I myself travel on the line, I cannot get a simple thing like tarts! I'll take this up with the chairman himself."

The chef called the waiter aside and said, "We can get him tarts at the next stop."

Right after the next stop the waiter was back again. "I'm happy to inform you, sir, that our chef has worked on these tarts especially for you. He hopes you like them. And with them, we would like to offer you this seventy-five-year-old brandy, compliments of the line."

The passenger threw his napkin on the table, made a fist, and shouted, "To hell with the tarts! I'd rather be angry!"

. . . (how empty our lives would be if we had nothing to resent) . . .

A man was a regular customer at a restaurant, and the management did its best to please him. So when he complained one day that only one piece of bread was being given him with his meal, the waiter promptly brought him four slices.

"That's good," he said, "but not good enough. I like bread—plenty of it."

So the next night he was given a dozen slices. "Good," he said. "But you're still being frugal, aren't you?"

Even a basketful of slices on the table next day did not stop his complaints.

So the manager decided to fix him. He had a colossal loaf

of bread baked specially for him. It was six feet long and three feet wide. The manager himself, with the help of two waiters, brought it in and laid it on an adjoining table, then waited for the reaction.

The man glared at the gigantic loaf, then looked at the manager, and said, "So we're back to one piece again!"

. . . (lighting a candle is good, but cursing the darkness is fun) . . .

A former inmate of a Nazi concentration camp was visiting a friend who had shared the ordeal with him.

"Have you forgiven the Nazis?" he asked his friend.

"Yes."

"Well, I haven't. I'm still consumed with hatred for them."

"In that case," said his friend gently, "they still have you in prison."

. . . (our enemies are not those who hate us but those whom we hate) . . .

❧

. . . and how proud they feel—generally for the wrong reasons— . . .

Friends of composer George Gershwin attempted to convey to his father the fact that *Rhapsody in Blue* was a work of genius.

"Of course, it is," said the old man. "It takes fifteen minutes to perform, doesn't it?"

. . . of their achievements!

A missionary, somewhere in the tropics, decided to impress his parishioners by taking some of them for a ride in a plane. The plane glided over their villages and hills and forests and rivers. Occasionally they would look out their windows but on the whole they did not seem to be one bit impressed.

Back on the ground his flock trooped out of the plane without a word of comment. Anxious to get some response, the missionary exclaimed, "Wasn't it wonderful? Think of what human beings have achieved! There we were, up in the sky, above the houses, above the trees, above the mountains, looking down on the earth!"

The group listened impassively. Finally, their leader spoke. "Insects can do it," he said.

"And what's more, they're happy."

After several thousand years we have advanced so much that we bolt our door and windows at night while the less "advanced" natives sleep in open huts.

✣

Said the psychologist to the client, "So sorry! I can help you change your behavior, but Nature takes her time and follows her own rhythm . . .

The captain of a submarine, desiring to test his engine room, asked for top speed then suddenly ordered an emergency stop. His orders were instantly obeyed.

The public address system was turned on. "This is the captain speaking. Well done, engine room. You stopped the sub in exactly 55.05 seconds."

Soon another voice boomed, "This is the chef. The sub may have stopped, but your steak and potatoes kept going. Cold dinner for everyone tonight!"

✣

. . . Moreover, I cannot really solve your problem . . .

The chief executive of a large company was greatly admired for his energy and drive. But he suffered from one embarrassing weakness: each time he entered the president's office to make his weekly report, he would wet his pants!

The kindly president advised him to see a proctologist. When he appeared before the president the following week, his pants were still wet! "Didn't you see the proctologist?" asked the president.

"No. He was out. I saw a psychologist instead. I'm cured. I no longer feel embarrassed!"

❧

. . . I can only exchange it for another . . .

Soon after World War II a London bus conductor noticed a passenger with a heavy parcel on his lap.

"What's that you have there?" he asked.

"An unexploded bomb that fell near my house. I'm taking it to the police station."

"Good God! You don't want to carry a thing like that on your lap, man! Put it under your seat!"

(The solution to a problem changes the problem.)

❧

. . . or intensify it."

Doctor to patient: "I've been treating you for guilt for the past ten years, and you are still feeling guilty about a trifle like that? You ought to feel ashamed of yourself!"

❧

A fellow went to a psychiatrist and was diagnosed as a workaholic. He had to take a second job to pay for the needed therapy.

Two little boys met.
   "How old are you?"
   "I'm five. How old are you?"
   "I don't know."
   "You don't know how old you are?"
   "Nope."
   "Do women bother you?"
   "Nope."
   "You're four."

A reporter was sent out to get the opinion of the man in the street about modern woman. The first person he ran into was a man who had just celebrated his one hundred and third birthday.

   "I'm afraid I won't be of much help to you, son," said the old man regretfully. "I quit thinking about women nearly two years ago!"

RELATIONSHIPS

Dialogue is the lifeblood of a relationship. But the obstacles to dialogue are many, alas, and those who surmont them, few.

Much is accomplished if, in the first place, we talk less and listen more . . .

President Theodore Roosevelt had a passion for big-game hunting. When he heard that a famous British hunter was visiting the States, he invited the man to the White House in the hope of getting some pointers from him.

After a two-hour meeting at which the two of them were closeted together and left undisturbed, the Englishman emerged looking somewhat dazed.

"What did you tell the President?" a reporter asked.

"I told him my name," said the worn-out visitor.

When Calvin Coolidge was President of the United States, he saw dozens of people each day. Most had complaints of one kind or another.

One day a visiting governor told the President that he

did not understand how he was able to meet so many people in the space of a few hours.

"Why, you are finished with all your visitors by dinnertime," said the governor, "while I am often in my office till midnight."

"Yes," said Coolidge. "That's because you talk."

❧

. . . and refrain from deciding ahead of time what the other is talking about . . .

A fourteen-year-old boy announced at dinner one evening that he had been chosen to teach his class the next day. His father, who was an expert in instructional methods for the military, seized this wonderful occasion to give his son the benefit of his own training and experience.

"This is the way we go about it in the Army, son," he said. "We first choose objectives made up of action, situation, and level of performance. Now decide ahead of time what *action* you want your students to perform, in what *situation* you want them to perform it, and finally, *how well* you wish them to perform. And remember, all education must be directed at performance, performance, performance."

The boy wasn't impressed. All he said was, "It won't work, Dad."

"Of course, it will. It always works. Why would it not work?"

"Because," said the young fellow. "I'm supposed to give a class on sex."

. . . and what the other wants . . .

Two trucks were standing back to back and a truck driver was struggling to get a huge crate from one truck to the other.

A passerby, seeing his desperate situation, volunteered to help. So the two of them huffed and puffed and struggled for well over half an hour with no result at all.

"I'm afraid it's no use," panted the passerby. "We'll never get it off this truck."

"Off!" yelled the driver. "Good God, I don't want it off. I want it on!"

. . . and not respond to what we assume the other said . . .

The village drunkard staggered up to the parish priest, newspaper in hand, and greeted him politely. The priest, annoyed, ignored the greeting because the man was slightly inebriated.

He had come with a purpose, however. "Excuse me, Father," he said, "could you tell me what causes arthritis?" The priest ignored that too.

But when the man repeated the question, the priest turned on him impatiently and cried, "Drinking causes arthritis, that's what! Gambling causes arthritis! Chasing loose women causes arthritis . . ." And only then, too late, he said, "Why did you ask?"

"Because it says right here in the papers that that's what the Pope has!"

⌇

. . . nor assume that we know what the other is talking about . . .

A storekeeper heard one of his salesman say to a customer, "No, ma'am, we haven't had any for some weeks now and it doesn't look as if we'll be getting any soon."

Horrified at what he was hearing, he rushed over to the customer as she was walking out and said, "That isn't true, ma'am. Of course, we'll have some soon. In fact, we placed an order for it a couple of weeks ago."

Then he drew the salesman aside and growled, "Never, never, never, never say we don't have something. If we don't have it, say we've ordered it and it's on its way. Now what was it she wanted?"

"Rain," said the salesman.

⌇

. . . nor put our own meaning into the other's words . . .

A reporter was interviewing a woman on her hundredth birthday. She seemed an extraordinarily vivacious sort of person who delighted in recalling her past. She had lived from the age of the covered wagon to the age of the supersonic jet; and she seemed eager to describe it all.

When the interview was over, she still seemed eager to talk, so the reporter tried to think up some question that would keep the conversation going. "Have you ever been bedridden?" he asked.

"Oh dear, yes," she said with a slight blush, "dozens of times. And twice in a haystack."

❧

. . . but frequently, alas, we don't even hear what the other is saying.

On their golden wedding anniversary, a couple were kept busy all day with the celebrations and the crowds of relatives and friends who dropped in to congratulate them. So they were grateful when, toward evening, they were able to be alone on the porch, watching the sunset and relaxing after the tiring day.

The old man gazed fondly at his wife and said, "Agatha, I'm proud of you!"

"What was that you said?" asked the old lady. "You know I'm hard of hearing. Say it louder."

"I said I'm proud of you."

"That's all right," she replied with a dismissive gesture. "I'm tired of you, too."

Perfect listening is listening not so much to others as to oneself. Perfect sight is seeing not others so much as oneself.

For they fail to understand the other who have not heard themselves; and they are blind to the reality of others who have not probed themselves. The perfect listener hears you even when you say nothing.

Woman to husband absorbed in newspaper: "You needn't bother saying 'uh-huh' anymore. I stopped talking ten minutes ago."

. . . and we hardly ever talk about the same things . . .

"Darling," said the wife, "I'm ashamed of the way we live. Father pays the rent for the house, Brother sends us food and money for clothes, Uncle pays our water and electricity bills, and our friends provide us with tickets for the theater. I'm not complaining really, but I do think we can do better."

"Of course, we can," said the husband. "I've been thinking about it myself lately. You've got a brother and two uncles who don't send us a cent!"

. . . do we?

Nasruddin's wife wanted a pet, so she bought a monkey.

Nasruddin wasn't pleased. "What's it going to eat?" he asked.

"Exactly what we eat," said the wife.

"And where is it going to sleep?"

"Right in bed with us."

"With us? What about the smell?"

"If I can put up with it, I guess the monkey can too."

The surest way to kill a relationship: insist on having things your way.

Johnny was a sturdy, robust kid of three. He made friends with a billy goat next door. Each morning he would pull up some grass and lettuce and take them over as breakfast for Billy. So deep was their friendship that Johnny would spend hours in Billy's pleasant company.

One day it occurred to Johnny that a change of diet would do Billy a lot of good. So he went to visit his friend with rhubarb instead of lettuce. Billy nibbled a bit of the rhubarb, decided he didn't want it, and pushed it away. Johnny caught Billy by one of his horns and attempted to get him to eat the rhubarb. This time Billy butted Johnny away, gently at first, but as Johnny grew persistent, quite firmly, so that Johnny stumbled and fell with a thump on his backside.

Johnny was so offended by this that he brushed himself off, glared at Billy, and walked away, never to return. Some days later when his father asked him why he never went over to chat with Billy, Johnny replied, "Because he rejected me."

All too frequently, we see people not as they are, but as we are.

An active young woman showed signs of stress and strain. The doctor prescribed tranquilizers and asked her to report to him after a couple of weeks.

When she came back he asked her if she felt any different. She said, "No. I don't. But I've observed that other people seem a lot more relaxed."

A woman complained to a visiting friend that her neighbor was a poor housekeeper. "You should see how dirty her children are—and her house. It is almost a disgrace to be living in the same neighborhood as her. Take a look at those clothes she has hung out on the line. See the black streaks on the sheets and towels!"

The friend walked up to the window and said, "I think the clothes are quite clean, my dear. The streaks are on your window."

A woman was at her singing lessons. She had such a jarring voice that a neighbor could take it no more. He managed, finally, to summon up the courage to knock at her door and say, "Madam, if you don't stop your singing I think I'll go mad!"

"What are you talking about?" said the woman. "I stopped two hours ago!"

So sorry! It isn't you I am dealing with but an image in my head.

Samuel was down in the dumps and who could blame him? His landlord had ordered him out of the apartment and he had nowhere to go. Suddenly light dawned. He could live with his good friend Moshe. The thought brought Samuel much comfort, until he was assailed by another thought that said, "What makes you so sure that Moshe will put you up at his place?" "Why wouldn't he?" said Samuel to the thought, somewhat heatedly. "After all, it is I who found him the place he is living in now; and it was I who advanced him the money to pay his rent for the first six months. Surely the least he could do is put me up for a week or so when I am in trouble."

That settled the matter until after dinner, when he was once again assailed by the thought: "Suppose he were to refuse?" "Refuse?" said Samuel. "Why in God's name would he refuse? The man owes me everything he has. It is

I who got him his job; it is I who introduced him to that lovely wife of his, who has borne him the three sons he glories in. Will he grudge me a room for a week? Impossible!"

That settled the matter until he got to bed and found he couldn't sleep because the thought came back to say, "But just suppose he were to refuse. What then?" This was too much for Samuel. "How the hell could he refuse?" he said, his temper rising now. "If the man is alive today, it is because of me. I saved him from drowning when he was a kid. Will he be so ungrateful as to turn me out into the streets in the middle of winter?"

But the thought was persistent. "Just suppose . . ." Poor Samuel struggled with it as long as he could. Finally he got out of bed around two in the morning, went over to where Moshe lived, and kept his finger pressed against the doorbell button till Moshe, half asleep, opened the door and said in astonishment, "Samuel! What is it? What brings you here in the middle of the night?" Samuel was so angry by now he couldn't keep himself from yelling, "I'll tell you what brings me here at this hour of the night! If you think I'm going to ask you to put me up even for a single day, you're mistaken. I don't want to have anything to do with you, your house, your wife, or your family. To hell with you all!" With that he turned on his heel and walked away.

❧

We see them mostly through the spectacles of our own preconceived notions.

BOSS: "You look exhausted. What happened?"
SECRETARY: "Well, I . . . No, you wouldn't believe me if I told you."
BOSS: "Of course I would."
SECRETARY: "No, you wouldn't. I know you wouldn't."
BOSS: "I really will believe you. I promise I will."
SECRETARY: "Well, I worked too hard today."
BOSS: "I don't believe it."

❧

A friend asked Nasruddin for a sum of money. Nasruddin was convinced the money wouldn't be returned. But since he did not want to offend the friend and the sum asked for was a small one, he gave him the money. To his great surprise, exactly one week after the loan was made, the man returned the money.

A month later he returned to ask for a slightly larger sum. Nasruddin refused. When the man asked why, he said, "Last time I did not expect you to return the money —and you let me down. This time I expect you to return it —I'm not going to be let down again!"

The defects we see in them are mostly our own.

"Excuse me, sir," said a timid student. "I couldn't make out what you wrote on the margin of my last paper."

"I told you to write more legibly," said the teacher.

"Darling," said a woman to her husband at a party, "you had better not have any more drinks. You're beginning to look blurred already."

Rare, indeed, is the relationship in which the other is not cultivated for what one can get for oneself.

"I hear you have broken your engagement with Tom. What happened?"

"Oh, my feelings toward him changed. That's what happened."

"Are you going to return his engagement ring?"

"Oh, no! My feelings toward the ring haven't changed."

❧

A young woman called a card shop. "Do you remember those wedding cards I ordered last week? Well, I was wondering if it is too late to make a few changes on them."

"Give me the new information, lady, and I'll check," said the shopkeeper.

"OK. It's a different date, a different church, and a different man."

It is quite impossible to be happily married to another if one does not first get a divorce from oneself.

❧

A farmer decided it was time he got married, so he saddled his mule and set off for the city to find himself a wife. In time, he met a woman he thought would make him a good wife and they were married.

After the ceremony they both climbed on to the mule and started back for the farm. After a while the mule stopped and refused to move, so the farmer dismounted and beat the mule with a huge stick until it started to move again. "That's one," said the farmer.

Some miles later the mule stopped again and once again the farmer dismounted and beat the mule till it started moving again. "That's two," said the farmer.

A few miles later the mule stopped a third time. This

time the farmer got down, got his wife down, took out his pistol, and shot the mule in the head, killing it instantly.

"You stupid, cruel man!" shouted his wife. "That was a good sturdy animal that could have been valuable on the farm and now, in a fit of temper, you have destroyed it. If I had known what a hard-hearted man you are, I would never have married you . . ." and so on, for nearly ten minutes.

The farmer heard her out till she paused for breath. Then he said, "That's one."

The story goes that they lived happily ever after.

"You look all in today, Jack, what's the trouble?"

"Well, I didn't get home until morning, and just as I was undressing, my wife woke up and said, 'Aren't you getting up pretty early, Jack?' So to avoid an argument, I put on my clothes and came back to work."

What price peace?

Two hippies, feeling high, were strolling down the street. Another hippie, walking toward them, gently lifted his hand in greeting and said, "Hi, there!"

Four blocks later, one hippie turned to the other and said, "Man, I thought he'd never stop talking!"

Reactions are relative . . .

. . . or are they?

A farm boy was so taciturn that his girl friend, after five years of courtship, decided that he was never going to propose to her and that she would have to take the initiative.

One day when they were sitting alone in the garden, she said to him, "John, let's get married. Shall we get married, John?"

A long silence followed. Finally John said, "Yes."

Another long silence. Finally the girl said, "Say something, John. Why don't you say something?"

"I'm afraid I've said too much already!"

❧

In ancient India, water used to be drawn out of wells by means of the Persian wheel, a convenient device whose only drawback was the great noise it made when in operation.

One day a horseman happened to pass by a farm and demanded water for his horse. The farmer gladly put the Persian wheel in motion but the horse, unaccustomed as it was to the noise, wouldn't come anywhere near the well.

"Can't you stop the noise so that my horse can drink?" asked the horseman.

"I'm afraid that isn't possible, sir," said the farmer. "If your horse wishes to drink, he will have to take the water with the noise, for water comes only with noise here."

And friendships come only with failings.

To relate is to react. To react is to understand oneself. To understand oneself is to be enlightened. Relationships are schools for enlightenment.

SERVICE

A farmer whose corn always took the first prize at the state fair had the habit of sharing his best corn seed with all the farmers in the neighborhood.

When asked why, he said, "It is really a matter of self-interest. The wind picks up the pollen and carries it from field to field. So if my neighbors grow inferior corn, the cross-pollination brings down the quality of my own corn. That is why I am concerned that they plant only the very best."

All that you give to others you are giving to yourself.

Once upon a time the members of the body were very annoyed with the stomach. They were resentful that they had to procure food and bring it to the stomach while the stomach itself did nothing but devour the fruit of their labor.

So they decided they would no longer bring the stomach food. The hands would not lift it to the mouth. The teeth would not chew it. The throat would not swallow it. That would force the stomach to do something.

But all they succeeded in doing was make the body weak to the point that they were all threatened with death. So it was finally they who learned the lesson that in helping one another they were really working for their own welfare.

It is impossible to help another without helping yourself, or to harm another without harming yourself.

Nasruddin was muttering to himself delightedly when his friend asked him what it was all about.

Said Nasruddin, "That idiot Ahmed keeps slapping me on the back each time he sees me. Well, I've put a stick of dynamite under my coat today, so this time when he slaps me he'll blow his arm off!"

Said a colonial governor to a native leader, "I deplore the oppression to which my people subject yours. You must help me solve the problem."

"Where's the problem?" asked the leader.

"Listen, my dear fellow. If I had you tied to a stake and lit a fire around you, you would have a problem, wouldn't you?"

"Would I? If you got me released, all would be well. If you let me burn, I would die. And you would have the problem!"

≈

A commuter hopped on to a train at New York and told the conductor he was going to Fordham. "We don't stop at Fordham on Saturdays," said the conductor, "but I'll tell you what I'll do. As we slow down at Fordham station, I shall open the door and you jump off. Make sure you're running along with the train when you hit the ground or you'll fall flat on your face."

At Fordham the door opened and the commuter hit the ground running forward. Another conductor, seeing him, opened the door and pulled him in as the train resumed speed. "You're mighty lucky, buddy," said the conductor. "This train doesn't stop at Fordham on Saturdays!"

In your own small way you can be of service to people—by getting out of their way.

There is the noble art of getting things done and the noble art of leaving things undone.

According to the newspapers, a heat wave was causing fainting spells, so a young lady was not surprised to see the middle-aged man next to her in church slump down toward the floor. Quickly she knelt down beside him, placed a firm hand on his head, and pushed it down between his knees. "Keep your head down," she whispered urgently. "You'll feel better if you get the blood into your head."

The man's wife looked on convulsed with laughter and

did nothing to help her husband or the young lady. She must be quite heartless, the young lady decided.

Then, to her dismay, the man managed to break loose from her muscular hold and hissed, "What are you up to, you meddling fool? I'm trying to retrieve my hat from under the bench!"

People who try to improve things frequently achieve remarkable success in making them worse.

In the final analysis the solution to problems lies neither in action nor in inaction but in understanding, for where there is true understanding, there is no problem.

A priest was walking down a street when he saw a little boy jumping up and down trying to ring a door bell. The poor kid was too small and the bell was too high.

So the priest went up and rang the bell for the little fellow. Then, turning to the kid with a smile, he asked, "What do we do now?"

The little fellow said, "Run like hell."

❧

A teacher asked her class of small pupils to tell about their acts of kindness to dumb animals.

There were several heart-stirring stories.

When it was Tommy's turn, he said proudly, "Well, I once kicked a boy for kicking a dog."

As well wage a war to end all wars or engage in violence that will lead to love.

Long ago, a rare bird, never seen before in China, alighted in the suburb of the capital city. The emperor was delighted. He ordered that food from his own table be offered to the bird and that his orchestra be brought in to play for its enjoyment.

But the bird looked miserable and dazed. It refused to touch any of the food offered to it and, in a short time, contracted a sickness and died.

A bird ate poisonous berries which did it no harm. One day it collected some for its meal and sacrificed a portion of its meal to feed its friend, a rabbit who, not wishing to seem ungrateful, ate the berries and died.

If the charge was one of breaking and entering with the intention of doing good, how many of us could plead Not Guilty?

A beggar saw a banker coming out of his office and said, "Could you give me a dime, sir, for a cup of coffee?"

The banker felt sorry for this man, who looked bedraggled and distraught. He said, "Here's a dollar. Take it and have ten cups of coffee."

The next day the beggar was there again at the steps of the banker's office and as the banker came out he punched him.

"Hey," said the banker. "What are you doing?"

"You and your lousy ten cups of coffee. They kept me awake the whole of last night!"

I confess to having helped you. Can you now find it in your heart to forgive me and let me go?

One day Nasruddin asked a wealthy man for some money.

"What do you want it for?"

"To buy an elephant."

"If you have no money, you will not be able to maintain the elephant."

"I asked for money," said Nasruddin, "not advice."

✺

A woman member of the ambulance brigade was on first-aid duty at the shore.

She noticed many empty bottles scattered over a grassy spot and was afraid that people might inadvertently step on them and hurt themselves. So she put down her first-aid kit and started picking up the bottles.

Then an elderly gentleman, distracted by what she was doing, tripped over her first-aid kit and hurt himself.

꒜

"Wake up, sir!" said the nurse, shaking the sleeping patient.

"What's the matter? What's gone wrong?" asked the startled patient.

"Nothing. I just forgot to give you your sleeping tablets."

We had a fire at our home yesterday. Fortunately it was put out before the fire department could do any damage.

꒜

I get a great kick out of serving you—but I still insist that you be grateful.

A bejeweled dowager stepped out of a fashionable hotel in London where she had been dining and dancing all evening at a charity ball for the support of street urchins.

She was about to get into her Rolls Royce when a street urchin walked up to her and whined, "Spare me sixpence, ma'am, for charity. I haven't eaten for two days."

The duchess recoiled from the kid. "You ungrateful wretch!" she exclaimed. "Don't you realize I have been dancing for you all night?"

Thank God our motives in serving others are hidden from the public eye.

The seaside concert was poor and got no reviews in the local papers. Attendance dropped sharply after the first performance. Yet one little man came every night and did not miss a single show. However, even his presence, gratifying as it was to the performers, could not keep the show afloat financially.

On the last night, the manager stepped before the curtain and said, "Ladies and gentlemen, before taking leave of you, we wish to thank our friend here in the front row for his much-valued patronage. He has not missed a single show!"

The little man rose to stammer his acknowledgment. "It's very decent of you," he said, "but as a matter of fact, this is the only place where my wife would never think of looking for me!"

"It was very kind of you to stay till the end of my speech when everyone else walked away!"

"Nice of you to say so. But I'm the next speaker, you see."

~~

Once upon a time there was an inn called the Silver Star. The innkeeper was unable to make ends meet even though he did his very best to draw customers by making the inn comfortable, the service cordial, and the prices reasonable. So in despair he consulted a sage.

After listening to his tale of woe, the sage said, "It is very simple. You must change the name of your inn."

"Impossible!" said the innkeeper. "It has been the Silver Star for generations and is well known all over the country."

"No," said the sage firmly. "You must now call it the Five Bells and have a row of six bells hanging at the entrance."

"Six bells? But that's absurd. What good would that do?"

"Give it a try and see," said the sage with a smile.

Well, the innkeeper gave it a try. And this is what he saw. Every traveler who passed by the inn walked in to point out the mistake, each one believing that no one else had noticed it. Once inside, they were impressed by the cordiality of the service and stayed on to refresh themselves, thereby providing the innkeeper with the fortune that he had been seeking in vain for so long.

There are few things the ego delights in more than correcting other people's mistakes.

❧

Once upon a time God gave a party for all the virtues, great and small, humble and heroic. They all gathered together in a splendidly decorated hall in heaven and soon began to enjoy themselves because they were well acquainted with one another; some were even closely related.

Suddenly God spotted two fair virtues who seemed not to know each other at all and were somewhat ill at ease in each other's company. So He took one of them by the hand and formally introduced her to the other. "Gratitude," He said, "this is Charity."

But God had hardly turned around when they were again parted. And so the story has gone around that even God cannot bring Gratitude to where Charity is.

❧

A group of newly arrived missionaries hired a native to take them for a canoe ride.

After a while they started hearing the steady beat of jungle drums. All along the route, at steady intervals, the sounds were repeated.

"What are the drums saying?" asked one of the missionaries fearfully.

The native guide listened to the drums and translated: "Drums say: Three white people. Very rich. Raise prices."

Saadi of Shiraj used to say, "No one learned archery from me who did not, in the end, make a target out of me."

A woman was leaning over the victim of a street accident and the crowd was looking on.

Suddenly she was roughly pushed aside by a man who said, "Step back, please. I've had a course in first aid."

The woman looked on for a few minutes while the man got busy with the victim. Then she said calmly, "When you come to the part where you have to send for the doctor, I'm already here!"

More often than you imagine, the doctor is already there— inside the person you are attempting to help!

So why bother with first aid? Summon the doctor!

An enthusiastic young priest was appointed chaplain of a hospital.

He was one day glancing through the admission cards of recently arrived patients and found one which stated that the patient was a Catholic.

There was also a curious note affixed to that card: "Does not want to see a priest unless she is unconscious."

Something to ask yourself each time you think you need help or advice: "Am I sure I'm conscious?"

A fire broke out in a house in which a man was fast asleep.

They tried to carry him out through the window. No way. They tried to carry him out through the door. No way. He was just too huge and heavy.

They were pretty desperate till someone suggested, "Wake him up, then he'll get out by himself."

Only sleepers and children need to be taken care of. Wake up! Or grow up!

A young man in training to be a priest was told that what people expect of a priest is that he listen to their woes. Just listen, listen, listen . . . Maybe he wouldn't be able to lend a helping hand, but he could always lend a sympathetic ear. So this is what he determined to do when he arrived at his first parish assignment.

No matter how much the whole of him revolted, he forced himself to listen, listen, listen . . . and the people were most appreciative. But something seemed to be going wrong somewhere. For instance, an old lady would come in and complain to a headache. Such a terrible, awful headache. "Tell me what's bothering you," the priest would say invitingly. So she would talk and talk and talk while the priest listened and listened and listened.

It always seemed to work. "I came in here an hour ago with such a headache, Father. And now it's gone, gone, gone."

And the priest would think, "I know, I know, I know. Because now I've got it!"

❧

A course on how to win friends and influence people was in progress. A young businessman was explaining to the class how he had applied all the principles of the course in an encounter with a business prospect. And it worked marvelously—well, almost!

"I did everything I was told to do here," he added. "I began by greeting him warmly, then I smiled at him and asked him about himself. I paid the closest attention to everything he said. I went out of my way to agree with his views and told him every now and then what a fine person I thought he was. He talked and talked for more than an hour. And when we finally parted company, I knew I had made a friend for life."

Everyone in the classroom applauded politely. When the applause died down, the speaker said with feeling, "But boy! What an enemy *he* made!"

Why make someone a gift you cannot emotionally afford to give?

❧

Old people are not lonely because they have no one to share their burden but because they have only their own burden to bear.

An eighty-five-year-old woman was being interviewed on her birthday. What advice would she have for people her age, the reporter asked.

"Well," said the old dear, "at our age it is very important to keep using all our potential or it dries up. It is important to be with people and, if it is at all possible, to earn one's living through service. That's what keeps us alive and well."

"May I ask what exactly you do for a living at your age?"

"I look after an old lady in my neighborhood," was her unexpected, delightful reply.

Love heals everyone—both those who receive it and those who give it.

❧

There is a story that before Moses led the people from the land of Egypt, he was apprenticed to a great master as a preparation for becoming a prophet. The first discipline that the master imposed on Moses was that of silence. The two of them wandered through the countryside one day and Moses was so dazzled by the beauties of nature that he found it easy to be silent. But when they got to the bank of a river, he saw a child drowning on the other shore and its poor mother crying aloud for help.

Moses could not keep silent before such a sight. "Master," he said, "can't you do something to save that child?" "Silence!" said the master. So Moses held his breath.

But his heart was troubled. He thought, "Can it be that this master of mine is really a hard-hearted, insensitive man? Or is he powerless to help those in need?" He was afraid to think such thoughts against his master, but he could not dispel them either.

In the course of their wandering they came to the seashore and saw a boat going down with all its crew. Moses said, "Master, look! That boat is sinking!" Once again the master bade him keep to his discipline of silence, so Moses did not speak any further.

But his heart was sorely troubled, so when they got back home he took the matter up with God, who said to him, "Your master was right. The child who was drowning was meant to bring about a war between two nations in which hundreds of thousands would have perished. This disaster was averted by his drowning. And as for that sinking ship, it was manned by pirates who were planning to make for a seaside town, there to pillage and plunder and massacre many innocent, peace-loving people."

Service is a virtue only when accompanied by wisdom.

The Ministry of Agriculture decreed that sparrows were a menace to the crops and should be exterminated.

When this was done, hoards of insects that the sparrows would have eaten descended on the harvest and began to ravage the crops, whereupon the Ministry of Agriculture came up with the idea of costly pesticides.

The pesticides made the food expensive. They also made it a hazard to health. Too late it was discovered that it was the sparrows who, though feeding on the crops, managed to keep the food wholesome and inexpensive.

There was once a man who had a golden belly button, but what to most people would have been a source of pride, to him was a source of embarrassment, for each time he took a shower or a swim he was the butt of his friend's teasing.

So he prayed and prayed that his belly button would be taken away. One night he dreamed that an angel came down from heaven, unscrewed his belly button, and went back to heaven.

When he woke in the morning the first thing he did was check to see if the dream was true. It was! There on the table lay the unscrewed belly button, all bright and shining. The man jumped out of bed in joy—and his bottom fell off!

Only the wise can be safely entrusted with the tasks of changing others or themselves.

❧

A woman in a village was surprised to find a fairly well-dressed stranger at her door asking for something to eat. "I'm sorry," she said. "I have nothing in the house right now."

"Not to worry," said the amiable stranger. "I have a soup stone in this satchel of mine; if you will let me put it in a pot of boiling water, I'll make the most delicious soup in the world. A very large pot, please."

The woman was curious. She put the pot on the fire and whispered the secret of the soup stone to a neighbor. By the time the water began to boil, all the neighbors had gathered to see the stranger and his soup stone. The stranger dropped the stone into the water then tasted a teaspoonful with relish and exclaimed, "Ah, delicious! All it needs is some potatoes."

"I have potatoes in my kitchen," shouted one woman. In a few minutes she was back with a large quantity of sliced potatoes, which were thrown into the pot. Then the stranger tasted the brew again. "Excellent!" he said. But added wistfully, "If we only had some meat, this would become a tasty stew."

Another housewife rushed home to bring some meat, which the stranger accepted graciously and flung into the pot. When he tasted the broth again, he rolled his eyes heavenward and said, "Ah, tasty! If we had some vegetables, it would be perfect, absolutely perfect."

One of the neighbors rushed off home and returned with a basketful of carrots and onions. After these had been thrown in too and the stranger tasted the mixture, he said in a voice of command, "Salt and sauce." "Right here," said the housewife. Then came another command: "Bowls for everyone." People rushed to their homes in search of bowls. Some even brought back bread and fruit.

Then they all sat down to a delicious meal while the stranger handed out large helpings of his incredible soup. Everyone felt strangely happy as they laughed and talked and shared their very first common meal. In the middle of the merriment the stranger quietly slipped away, leaving behind the miraculous soup stone, which they could use anytime they wanted to make the loveliest soup in the world.

A great festival was to be held in a village and each villager was asked to contribute by pouring a bottle of wine into a giant barrel. One of the villagers had this thought: "If I pour a bottle of water in that giant barrel, no one will notice the difference." But it didn't occur to him that everyone else in the village might have the same thought. When the banquet began and the barrel was tapped, what came out of it was pure water.

~∂

A tale from the Fathers of the Egyptian Desert:

There was an old hermit, very ascetical in body and holy in spirit, but somewhat unclear in his thoughts. This man went to see Abba John to ask him about forgetfulness. Having received a word of wisdom, he returned to his cell. But on the way back he forgot what Abba John had told him.

So he went back and got the same word. But once again, on the way back to his cell, he forgot it. This happened several times. He would listen to Abba John and, on his way back to the cell, would be overcome by forgetfulness.

Many days later he happened to meet Abba John and he said, "Do you know, Father, that I have once again forgotten what you told me? I would have come back again but I have been enough of a bother to you already and do not want to overburden you."

Abba John said to him, "Go and light a lamp." The old man lit the lamp. Then John said, "Bring in some more lamps and light them from the first one." This, too, the old man did.

Then Abba John said to the old man, "Did the first lamp suffer any loss from the fact that the other lamps were lit from it?"

"No," said the old man.

"Well, then, so it is with me. If not only you but the whole town of Scetis were to come to me to seek help or advice, I would not suffer the slightest loss. So come to me whenever you wish, without any hesitation."

❧

A disciple came up to his master and said, "I am a wealthy man and have just come into a large fortune. How best can I use it so it will redound to my spiritual benefit?"

Said the master, "Come back after a week and I shall give you an answer."

When he returned, the master said with a sigh, "I am at a loss what to say to you. If I tell you to give it to your friends and relatives, it will do you no spiritual good. If I tell you to give it to the temple, you will only feed the avarice of the priests. And if I tell you to give it to the poor, you will take pride in your charity and fall into the sin of self-righteousness."

Since the disciple pressed the master for an answer, he finally said, "Give the money to the poor. At least they will benefit from it, even though you will not."

If you do not serve, you injure others. If you do, you injure yourself. Ignorance of this dilemma is the death of the soul. Freedom from this dilemma is eternal life.

❧

Another tale from the Fathers of the Desert:

A brother once put this question to one of the elders: "There are two brothers, one of whom remains praying in his cell, fasting six days a week, and practicing much austerity. The other spends all his time taking care of the sick. Which one's work is more pleasing to God?"

The elder replied, "If the brother who fasts and prays were to hang himself up by the nose, he would not equal even one act of kindness of the one who takes care of the sick."

There was once a man who was busy building a home for himself. He wanted it to be the nicest, cosiest home in the world.

Someone came to him to ask for help because the world was on fire. But it was his home he was interested in, not the world.

When he finally finished his home, he found he did not have a planet to put it on.

A schoolteacher gave up teaching for social work. When his friend wanted to know why, this is what he had to say:

"Little can be done in school if nothing is done in the home and the world. At school I felt like a man who was searching for ivory in the forest. When he finally found it, he discovered it was attached to a large elephant."

Wife to husband whose face is buried in the newspaper: "Has it ever occurred to you that there might be more to life than what's going on in the world."

Most people love humanity. It's the person next door they cannot stand.

ENLIGHTENMENT

Once upon a time there was a stonecutter. Each day he went up to the mountains to cut stones. And while he worked he sang, for though he was a poor man, he desired no more than he had, so he had not a care in the world.

One day he was called to work on the mansion of a nobleman. When he saw the magnificence of the mansion, he experienced the pain of desire for the first time in his life and he said with a sigh, "If only I were rich! Then I would not have to earn my living in sweat and toil as I do now."

Imagine his astonishment when he heard a voice say, "Your wish has been granted. Henceforth, anything you desire will be given to you." He did not know what to make of the words till he returned to his hut that evening and found in its place a mansion as magnificent as the one he had been working on. So the stonecutter gave up cutting stones and began to enjoy the life of the rich.

One day when the afternoon was hot and humid, he happened to look out his window and saw the King go by with a large retinue of noblemen and slaves. He thought, "How I wish I were a King myself, sitting in the cool of the royal carriage!" His wish was promptly carried out and he found himself reclining in the comfort of the royal carriage. But the carriage turned out to be warmer than he had assumed it to be. He looked out of the carriage window and began to marvel at the power of the sun, whose heat could penetrate even the thick walls of the carriage. "I wish I were the sun," he said to himself. Once again his wish was granted and he found himself sending out waves of heat into the universe.

All went well for a while. Then on a rainy day, he attempted to pierce through a thick bank of clouds and could not. So he got himself changed into a cloud and glorified in his power to keep the sun away—till he turned into rain and found, to his annoyance, a mighty rock that blocked his path so he was obliged to flow around it.

"What?" he cried. "A mere rock more powerful than I? Well, then I wish to be a rock." So there he was standing tall upon a mountainside. He barely had time to rejoice in his fine figure, however, when he heard strange clipping sounds proceeding from his feet. He looked down and, to his dismay, found a tiny human being sitting there engaged in cutting chunks of stone from his feet.

"What?" he shouted. "A puny creature like that more powerful than an imposing rock like me? I want to be a man!" So he found he was once again a stonecutter going up into the mountain to cut stone, earning his living in sweat and toil but with a song in his heart because he was content to be what he was and to live by what he had.

Nothing is as good as it seems before we get it.

Every month the disciple faithfully sent his master an account of his spiritual progress.

In the first month he wrote, "I feel an expansion of consciousness and experience my oneness with the universe." The master glanced at the note and threw it away.

The following month this is what he had to say: "I have finally discovered that the divine is present in all things." The master seemed disappointed.

In his third letter the disciple enthusiastically explained, "The mystery of the One and the many has been revealed to my wondering gaze." The master yawned.

His next letter said, "No one is born, no one lives, and no one dies, for the self is not." The master threw his hands up in despair.

After that a month passed by, then two, then five; then a whole year. The master thought it was time to remind his disciple of his duty to keep him informed of his spiritual progress. The disciple wrote back, "Who cares?" When the master read those words, a look of satisfaction spread over his face. He said, "Thank God, at last he's got it!"

Even the hankering for freedom is a bondage. Are you ever truly free till it no longer matters to you if you are free or not?

Only the content are free.

❧

A great and foolish King complained that the rough ground hurt his feet, so he ordered the whole country to be carpeted with cowhide.

The court jester laughed when the King told him of his order. "What an absolutely crazy idea, Your Majesty," he cried. "Why all the needless expense? Just cut out two small pads to protect your feet!"

That is what the king did. And that is how the idea of shoes was born.

The enlightened know that to make the world a painless place, you need to change your heart—not the world.

Wolves were discovered in the village near Master Shoju's temple, so each night for a whole week Shoju went to the village cemetery and sat there in meditation. This put an end to the nightly attacks of the wolves.

The villagers were ecstatic. They begged him to reveal to them the secret rites he had performed so that they could do the same in the future.

Said Shoju, "I did not have to resort to secret rites. While I sat there in meditation a number of wolves gathered around me. They licked the tip of my nose and sniffed my windpipe. But because I remained in the right state of mind, I wasn't bitten."

A maharaja went out to sea when a great storm arose. One of the slaves on board began to cry out and wail in fear, for the man had never been on a ship before. His crying was so loud and so prolonged that everyone on board began to be annoyed and the maharaja was for throwing the man overboard.

But his chief advisor, who was a sage, said, "No. Let me deal with the man. I think I can cure him."

With that he ordered some of the sailors to hurl the man into the sea. The moment he found himself in the sea the poor slave began to scream in terror and to thrash out wildly. In a few seconds the sage ordered him to be hauled on board.

Back on board the slave lay in a corner in absolute silence. When the maharaja asked his advisor for the reason, he replied, "We never realize how lucky we are till our situation gets worse."

During the Second World War a man was adrift on a raft for twenty-one days before he was rescued.

Asked if he had learned anything from the experience he replied, "Yes. If I can only have an abundance of food to eat and plenty of water to drink, I shall be riotously happy for the rest of my life."

An old man says he complained only once in all his life—
when his feet were bare and he had no money to buy shoes.
  Then he saw a happy man who had no feet. And he never
complained again.

ॐ

The present moment is never unbearable if you live in it
fully. What is unbearable is to have your body here at 10
A.M. *and your mind at 6* P.M.; *your body in Bombay and*
your mind in San Francisco.

The clock master was about to fix the pendulum of a clock
when, to his surprise, he heard the pendulum speak.

"Please, sir, leave me alone," the pendulum pleaded. "It
will be an act of kindness on your part. Think of the number of times I will have to tick day and night. So many
times each minute, sixty minutes an hour, twenty-four
hours a day, three hundred and sixty-five days a year. For
year upon year . . . millions of ticks. I could never do it."

But the clock master answered wisely, "Don't think of
the future. Just do one tick at a time and you will enjoy
every tick for the rest of your life."

And that is exactly what the pendulum decided to do. It
is still ticking merrily away.

❧

Here is a parable that the Lord Buddha told his disciples:

A man came across a tiger in a field. The tiger gave chase and the man fled. He came upon a precipice, stumbled, and began to fall. Then he reached out and caught hold of a little strawberry bush that was growing along the side of the precipice. There he hung for some minutes, suspended between the hungry tiger above and the deep chasm below, where he was soon going to meet his death.

Suddenly he spied a luscious strawberry growing on the bush. Grasping the bush with one hand, he plucked the strawberry with the other and put it into his mouth. Never in his life had a strawberry tasted so sweet!

To the enlightened the awareness of death gives sweetness to life.

The nervous tourist was afraid to get too close to the cliff. "What would I do," he said to the guide, "if I fell over the edge?"

"In that case, sir," said the guide enthusiastically, "don't fail to look to the right. You'll love the view!"

Only if you, too, are enlightened, of course!

❧

There was a crowd in the doctor's waiting room. An elderly gentleman rose and approached the receptionist.

"Madam," he said courteously, "my appointment was for ten o'clock and it is almost eleven now. I cannot wait any longer. Would you kindly give me an appointment for another day?"

One woman in the crowd leaned over to another and said, "He must be at least eighty years old. What sort of urgent business can he have that he cannot afford to wait?"

The man overheard the whispered remark. He turned to the lady, bowed, and said, "I am eighty-seven years old, ma'am. Which is precisely the reason why I cannot afford to waste a single minute of the precious time I have left."

The enlightened do not waste a minute because they have understood the relative unimportance of everything they do.

❧

Socrates was in prison awaiting his execution. One day he heard a fellow prisoner singing a difficult lyric by the poet Stesichoros.

Socrates begged the man to teach him the lyric.

"Why?" asked the singer.

"So that I can die knowing one thing more," was the great man's reply.

DISCIPLE: *Why learn something new one week before you die?*

MASTER: *For exactly the same reason that you would learn something new fifty years before you die.*

❧

Tajima no Kami was fencing master to the Shogun.

One of the Shogun's bodyguards came to him one day asking to be trained in swordsmanship.

"I have watched you carefully," said Tajima no Kami, "and you seem to be a master in the art yourself. Before taking you on as a pupil, I request you to tell me what master you studied under."

The bodyguard replied, "I have never studied the art under anyone."

"You cannot fool me," said the teacher. "I have a discerning eye and it never fails."

"I do not mean to contradict your excellency," said the guard, "but I really do not know a thing about fencing."

The teacher engaged the man in swordplay for a few minutes then stopped and said, "Since you say you have never learned the art, I take your word for it. But you are some kind of master. Tell me about yourself."

"There is one thing," said the guard. "When I was a child I was told by a samurai that a man should never fear death. I therefore struggled with the question of death till it ceased to cause me the slightest anxiety."

"So that's what it is," cried Tajima no Kami. "The ulti-

mate secret of swordsmanship lies in being free from the
fear of death. You need no training. You are a master in
your own right."

*The unenlightened are always anxious. Like the man in the
river who doesn't know how to swim. He becomes frightened. So he sinks. So he struggles to keep afloat. So he sinks
even deeper. If he dropped his fear and allowed himself to
sink, his body would come up to the surface on its own.*

*There was once a man who fell into a stream while he was
having an epileptic fit. When he came to later, he was surprised to find himself lying on the bank. The fit that had
thrown him into the river had also saved his life by removing
his fear of drowning . . . that's enlightenment.*

Kenji was a Japanese kamikaze pilot. He had prepared himself to die for his country but the war ended sooner than
expected and he never got his chance to die with honor. So
the man became depressed; he lost all appetite for living
and wandered listlessly around town, unsure what to do
with himself.

One day he was told of a thief who was holding an old
woman hostage in her apartment on the second floor of a
building. The police were afraid to move into the apartment because the man was armed and known to be dangerous.

Kenji rushed into the building and demanded that the
man release the woman. A fight with knives ensued in

which Kenji killed the thief but he was mortally wounded himself. He died a little later in hospital with a contented smile on his lips. His wish to die a useful death had been fulfilled.

Only those do Good who have lost their fear to die.

There was once a huge dragon in China who went from village to village killing cattle and dogs and chicken and children indiscriminately. So the villagers called upon a wizard to help them in their distress. The wizard said, "I cannot slay the dragon myself, for magician though I am, I am too afraid. But I shall find you the man who will."

With that he transformed himself into a dragon and took up position on a bridge so everyone who did not know it was the wizard was afraid to pass. One day, however, a traveler came up to the bridge, calmly climbed over the dragon, and walked on.

The wizard promptly took on human shape again and called to the man, "Come back, my friend. I have been standing here for weeks waiting for you!"

The enlightened know that fear is in the way you look at things, not in the things themselves.

❧

A King ran into a dervish, and in keeping with the custom of the East when a King met a subject, he said, "Ask for a favor."

The dervish replied, "It would be unseemly for me to ask a favor of one of my slaves."

"How dare you speak so disrespectfully to the King," said a guardsman. "Explain yourself or you shall die."

The dervish said, "I have a slave who is the master of your King."

"Who?"

"Fear," said the dervish.

When the body perishes, life is no more. Hence the erroneous conclusion that to keep the body alive is the same as living.

Enter where the assassin's bullet does not take life away; neither does the prolongation of life lengthen the duration of one's being.

❧

When the Greek philosopher Diogenes was captured and taken to be sold in the slave market, it is said that he mounted the auctioneer's platform and cried aloud, "A master has come here to be sold. Is there some slave among you who is desirous of purchasing him?"

It is impossible to make slaves of the enlightened, for they are just as happy in a state of slavery as in a state of freedom.

❧

A merchant in Baghdad sent his servant on an errand to the bazaar and the man came back white with fear and trembling. "Master," he said, "while I was in the market-place, I walked into a stranger. When I looked him in the face, I found that it was Death. He made a threatening gesture at me and walked away. Now I am afraid. Please give me a horse so that I can ride at once so Samarra and put as great a distance as possible between Death and me."

The merchant—in his anxiety for the man—gave him his swiftest steed. The servant was on it and away in a trice.

Later in the day the merchant himself went down to the bazaar and saw Death loitering there in the crowd. So he went up to him and said, "You made a threatening gesture at my poor servant this morning. What did it mean?"

"That was no threatening gesture, sir," said Death. "It was a start of surprise at seeing him here in Baghdad."

"Why would he not be in Baghdad? This is where the man lives."

"Well, I had been given to understand that he would join me in Samarra tonight, you see."

Most people are so afraid to die that, from their efforts to avoid death, they never live.

❧

There was once a holy man who lived in a state of ecstasy but was regarded by everyone as insane. One day, having begged for food in the village, he sat by the roadside and began to eat when a dog came up and looked at him hungrily. The holy man then began to feed the dog; he himself would take a morsel, then give a morsel to the dog as though he and the dog were old friends. Soon a crowd gathered around the two of them to watch this extraordinary sight.

One of the men in the crowd jeered at the holy man. He said to the others, "What can you expect from someone so insane that he is not able to distinguish between a human being and a dog?"

The holy man replied, "Why do you laugh? Do you not see Vishnu seated with Vishnu? Vishnu is being fed and Vishnu is doing the feeding. So why do you laugh, oh Vishnu?"

❧

The Lord Krishna said to Arjun, "You speak of me as of an incarnation of God. But today I wish to reveal something special to you. Follow me."

Arjun followed the Lord a short distance. Then Krishna pointed to a tree and said, "What do you see there?"

Arjun replied, "A huge vine with clusters of grapes hanging on it."

The Lord said, "Those are not grapes. Go closer and look at them carefully."

When Arjun did that, he could hardly believe his eyes for there before him were Krishnas hanging in bunches from Krishna.

The disciples asked the master to speak to them of death: "What will it be like?"

"It will be as if a veil is ripped apart and you will say in wonder, 'So it was You all along!'"

There was once a King in India who had an elephant that ran amuck. It marched from village to village destroying everything in its path and no one dared attack it because it belonged to the King.

Now one day a self-styled ascetic was about to set out from a village when all the villagers begged him not to, because the elephant had been sighted on the road and was attacking passersby.

The man rejoiced in the occasion he now had for demonstrating his superior wisdom, for he had just returned from a lecture given by his guru, who had taught him to see Rama in everything. "Oh, you poor ignorant fools!" he said. "Have you no insight at all into spiritual matters? Have you never been told that we must see Rama in everyone and everything and that all those who do so will enjoy the protection of Rama? Let me go. I have no fear of the elephant."

The people thought that the man was about as spiritually insightful as the mad elephant. They knew it was useless to argue with a holy man, so they let him go. He had hardly got onto the road when the elephant rushed toward him, lifted him up with its trunk, and hurled him against a tree. The man began to howl in pain. To his good luck the King's guards appeared in the nick of time and captured the elephant before it could kill the deluded ascetic.

It was many months later before the man was well enough to set out on his travels again. He went straight to his guru and said, "The teaching you gave me was false. You told me to see everything as being pervaded by Rama. That is exactly what I did and look what happened!"

Said the guru, "How foolish you are! Why did you fail to see Rama in the villagers who warned you against the elephant?"

There was once a candymaker who made candy in the shapes of animals and birds of different colors and sizes. When he sold his candy to children, they would begin to quarrel with words such as these: "My rabbit is better than your tiger . . . My squirrel may be smaller than your elephant, but it is tastier . . ."

And the candymaker would laugh at the thought of grown-ups who were no less ignorant than the children when they thought that one person was better than another.

Enlightenment knows that it is our culture and conditioning, not our nature, that divides us.

A shepherd was grazing his sheep when a passerby said, "That's a fine flock of sheep you have. Could I ask you something about them?" "Of course," said the shepherd. Said the man, "How much would you say your sheep walk each day?" "Which ones, the white ones or the black ones?" "The white ones." "Well, the white ones walk about four miles a day." "And the black ones?" "The black ones too."

"And how much grass would you say they eat each day?" "Which ones, the white or the black?" "The white ones." "Well, the white ones eat about four pounds of grass each day." "And the black ones?" "The black ones too." "And how much wool would you say they give each year?" "Which ones, the white or the black?" "The white ones." "Well, I'd say the white ones give some six pounds of wool each year at shearing time." "And the black ones?" "The black ones too."

The passerby was intrigued. "May I ask you why you have this strange habit of dividing your sheep into white and black each time you answer one of my questions?" "Well," said the shepherd, "that's only natural. The white ones are mine, you see." "Ah! And the black ones?" "The black ones too," said the shepherd.

The human mind makes foolish divisions in what Love sees as One.

Plutarch tells the story of how Alexander the Great came upon Diogenes looking attentively at a heap of human bones.

"What are you looking for?" asked Alexander.

"Something that I cannot find," said the philosopher.

"And what is that?"

"The difference between your father's bones and those of his slaves."

The following are just as indistinguishable: Catholic bones from Protestant bones, Hindu from Muslim bones, Arab bones from Israeli bones, Russian bones from American bones.

The enlightened fail to see the difference even when the bones are clothed in flesh!

In a little Indian village lived a weaver who was a very pious soul. All day long he would pronounce the name of God and people trusted him implicitly. When he had woven a sufficient amount of cloth, he would take it to be sold in the marketplace. There, if anyone asked him the price of a piece of cloth, he would reply in this fashion: "By the will of Rama the price of the yarn is thirty-five cents; the labour is ten cents; the profit, by the will of Rama, is four cents. So the price of this piece, by the will of Rama, is forty-nine cents." People had such faith in the man that they never bargained with him; they just paid the price he asked for and took the cloth.

Now the weaver was in the habit of going to the village temple at night to chant the praises of God and sing the glories of His name. Late one night, while he was at his chanting, a band of robbers burst in. They needed someone to carry their stolen goods for them so they said, "Come with us." The weaver meekly accompanied them with the goods on his head. Soon the police gave chase and the robbers began to run; the weaver ran with them, but since he was an older man, the police soon caught up with him, and finding the stolen goods on him, they arrested him and threw him in jail.

The following morning he was sent before the judge and accused of burglary. When the judge asked him what he had to say for himself, this is what the man said: "Your honor, by the will of Rama I finished my meal last night and by the will of Rama I went over to the temple, there to chant his praises. That is when suddenly, by the will of Rama, a band of robbers burst in and, by Rama's will, invited me to carry their goods for them. They put such a load on my head that when, by the will of Rama, the police gave chase, I was easily caught. Then, by the will of Rama, I was arrested and thrown in jail. And here I am standing before you this morning, by the will of Rama."

The judge said to the policeman, "Let the man go. He is evidently out of his mind."

Back home when asked what had happened, the pious weaver said, "By the will of Rama I was arrested and tried in court. And by the will of Rama I have been acquitted."

There was a rabbi who lived in a village on the steppes of Russia. Every morning for twenty years he crossed the village square to pray in the synagogue and every morning he was closely watched by a policeman who hated Jews.

Finally one morning the policeman walked up to the rabbi and demanded to know where he was going.

"I don't know," said the rabbi.

"What do you mean you don't know? For the past twenty years I have seen you go to that synagogue across the square and now you say you don't know? I'll teach you a lesson!"

With that he grabbed the old man by his beard and dragged him off to jail. As the policeman was turning the key on the prison cell, the rabbi looked at him with a twinkle in his eye and said, "See what I meant when I said I didn't know?"

TRAVELER: "What kind of weather are we going to have today?"

SHEPHERD: "The kind of weather I like."

TRAVELER: "How do you know it will be the kind of weather you like?"

SHEPHERD: "Having found out, sir, I cannot always get what I like, I have learned always to like what I get. So I am quite sure we will have the kind of weather I like."

Happiness and unhappiness are in the way we meet events, not in the nature of those events themselves.

❧

An old nun who had tried out the new habit was discussing her funeral with the Mother Superior.

"I'd like to be buried in the old habit," she said.

"Of course," said the Superior, "if you'll be more comfortable in that!"

When the self is no more, one has died—and like a corpse, one is comfortable in anything.

After all, someone whose mind is set on drowning does not insist on a set of dry clothes to make the drowning more agreeable.

❧

A Hasidic tale:

One night Rabbi Isaac was told in his dream to go to faraway Prague and there to dig for hidden treasure under a bridge that led to the palace of the King. He did not take the dream seriously, but when it recurred four or five times, he made up his mind to go in search of the treasure.

When he got to the bridge, he discovered to his dismay that it was heavily guarded day and night by soldiers. All he could do was gaze at the bridge from a distance. But since he went there every morning, the captain of the guards came up to him one day to find out why. Rabbi Isaac, embarrassed as he was to tell his dream to another soul, told the captain everything, for he liked the good-natured character of this Christian.

The captain roared with laughter and said, "Good heavens! You a rabbi and you take dreams so seriously? Why, if I were stupid enough to act on my own dreams, I would be wandering around in Poland today. Let me tell you one that I had last night that keeps recurring frequently: A voice tells me to go to Krakow and dig for treasure in the corner of the kitchen of one Isaac, son of Ezechiel! Now wouldn't it be the most stupid thing in the world to search around in Krakow for a man called Isaac and another called Ezechiel when half the male population there probably has one name and the other half the other?"

The Rabbi was stunned. He thanked the captain for his advice, hurried home, dug up the corner of his kitchen, and found a treasure abundant enough to keep him in comfort till the day he died.

The spiritual quest is a journey without distance. You travel from where you are right now to where you have always been. From ignorance to recognition, for all you do is see for the first time what you have always been looking at.

Who ever heard of a path that brings you to yourself or a method that makes you what you have always been? Spirituality, after all, is only a matter of becoming what you really are.

A young man became obsessed with a passion for Truth so he took leave of his family and friends and set out in search of it. He traveled over many lands, sailed across many oceans, climbed many mountains, and all in all, went through a great deal of hardship and suffering.

One day he awoke to find he was seventy-five years old and had still not found the Truth he had been searching for. So he decided, sadly, to give up the search and go back home.

It took him months to return to his hometown for he was an old man now. Once home, he opened the door of his house—and there he found that Truth had been patiently waiting for him all those years.

QUESTION: Did his journeying help him to find Truth?
ANSWER: No, but it prepared him to recognize it.

❧

A woman tourist from the West was admiring a native's necklace.

"What is it made of?" she asked.

"Alligator teeth, ma'am," said the native.

"Oh, I see. I suppose they have the same value for you people that pearls have for us."

"Not quite. Anyone can open an oyster."

The enlightened understand that a diamond is a stone until endowed with value by the human mind.

And that things are as big or as small as your mind chooses to make them.

A young American got a clerical job at the White House and had just participated in a reception given to all White House staffers by the President. He thought his mother would be thrilled to get a call from the White House, so he placed a call through the White House switchboard.

"Mother," he said proudly, "this is a big day for me. You know what? I am calling you from the White House."

The response he got from the other end was not quite as excited as he had expected it to be. Toward the end of the conversation his mother said, "Well, son, it's been a big day for me too."

"Really? What happened?"

"I finally managed to clean out the attic."

❧

The unenlightened fail to see themselves as the cause of all their griefs.

It was lunchtime at the factory and a workman opened his lunch box dolefully. "Oh, no," he said aloud. "Cheese sandwiches again!"

This happened a second and a third and a fourth day. Then a co-worker who had heard the mutterings of the man said, "If you hate cheese sandwiches so much, why don't you get your wife to make some other type?"

"Because I'm not married. I make those sandwiches myself."

❧

John and Mary were walking down the road in the late evening.

"I'm terribly afraid, John," said Mary.

"And what would you be afraid of?"

"I'm afraid you might be going to kiss me."

"And how would I kiss you with me carrying a bucket in each hand and a hen under each arm?"

"I was afraid that you might put a hen under each bucket and then kiss me."

More often than you think, what people do to you is what you've asked them to!

❧

A couple of soldiers in northern India were on their way back home in a rickshaw when they saw, ahead of them, another rickshaw with a couple of sailors in it.

In a few minutes the rivalry between the services erupted into a race in which the driver of the soldiers' rickshaw took an early lead.

They were settling back to savor their victory when, to their amazement, they saw their opponents shoot by. They were even more astonished to see the driver in the passenger seat lustily cheering one of the sailors, who had taken over from him.

The enlightened would rather be contented than victorious.

Two gunfighters were about to engage in a duel, and a space was cleared for them in the saloon. One was an unimposing tiny little man, but a professional fighter. The other was a huge, hefty fellow who protested, "Wait a minute! This isn't fair. He's shooting a larger target."

The little fellow was quick to offer a suggestion. Turning to the saloon owner he said, "Chalk out a man of my size on my opponent. Any bullet of mine that hits outside the line doesn't count."

The enlightened care more about living than about winning.

The unenlightened would sell their souls to prove they are right!

"Before I go out in the evening, I bet my wife ten dollars that I'll be back by midnight."

"And then?"

"And then I let her win."

An infallible sign of enlightenment: one no longer cares what other people think and say.

A furniture company sent this note to one of its customers:

> Dear Mr. Jones,
> What would your neighbors think if we had to send a truck to your house to repossess the furniture that you still have not paid for?

They got the following reply:

> Dear Sir,
> I have discussed the matter with my neighbors to find out what they would think. They all think it would be a dirty trick of a mean, low-down company.

A man grew up with the conviction that he would be satisfied with nothing but the very best. This conviction helped him to become very successful and very rich, so he now had the means with which to provide himself with nothing but the best.

Now it happened that he was suffering from a severe attack of tonsilitis, a condition that could have been dealt with effectively by any qualified surgeon in the land. But impressed as he was with a sense of his own importance, and goaded by his obsession to provide himself with the very best that the medical world had to offer, he began to move from one town to another, one country to another, in search of the best man for the job.

Each time some particularly competent surgeon was recommended to him, he began to fear that there might just possibly be someone who was even more competent.

One day his condition became so bad and his throat so infected that an operation had to be performed immediately, for his life was in danger. But the man was in a semicomatose state in a godforsaken village where the only person who had used a knife on a living creature was the village butcher.

He was a remarkably good butcher and went to work with a will, but when he got to the man's tonsils, he didn't quite know what he was supposed to do with them. And while he was busy consulting people who knew as little as he, the poor patient for whom nothing but the very best was good enough bled to death.

A lion was taken into captivity and thrown into a concentration camp where, to his amazement, he found other lions who had been there for years, some of them all their lives, for they had been born there. He soon became acquainted with the social activities of the camp lions. They banded themselves into groups. One group consisted of the socializers; another was into show business; another was cultural, for its purpose was to carefully preserve the customs, the tradition, and the history of the times when lions were free; other groups were religious—they gathered mostly to sing moving songs about a future jungle where there would be no fences; some groups attracted those who were literary and artistic by nature; others still were revolutionary, and they met to plot against their captors or against other revolutionary groups. Every now and then a revolution would break out, one particular group would be wiped out by another, or the guards would all be killed and replaced by another set of guards.

As he looked around, the newcomer observed one lion who always seemed deep in thought, a loner who belonged to no group and mostly kept away from everyone. There was something strange about him that commanded everyone's admiration and everyone's hostility, for his presence aroused fear and self-doubt. He said to the newcomer, "Join no group. These poor fools are busy with everything except what is essential."

"And what is that?" asked the newcomer.

"Studying the nature of the fence."

Nothing—but nothing—else matters!

The human condition is perfectly depicted in the case of the poor drunk standing late at night outside the park, beating on the fence, and yelling, "Let me out!"

Only your illusions prevent you from seeing that you are— and always have been—free.

❧

A basic ingredient in the attainment of freedom: adversity that brings awareness.

A traveler lost in the desert despaired of ever finding water. He struggled up one hilltop then another and another in the hope of sighting a stream somewhere. He kept looking in every direction with no success.

As he staggered onward, his foot caught on a dry bush and he stumbled to the ground. That's where he lay, with no energy even to rise, no desire to struggle anymore, no hope of surviving this ordeal.

As he lay there, helpless and dejected, he suddenly became aware of the silence of the desert. On all sides a majestic stillness reigned, undisturbed by the slightest sound. Suddenly he raised his head. He had heard something. Something so faint that only the sharpest ear and the deepest silence would lead to its detection: the sound of running water.

Heartened by the hope that the sound aroused in him, he rose and kept moving till he arrived at a stream of fresh, cool water.

❧

There isn't any world other than this one. But there are two ways of looking at it.